Air Force Colors

Volume 3

Pacific and Home Front, 1942-47

By Dana Bell

Illustrated by Don Greer

Betty Stadt and **Dana Bell**

  squadron/signal publications

P-47Ns out of Ie Shima wear the yellow wing bands and tails of the 507th Fightr Group with the blue triangles of the 463rd Fighter Squadron.

Dedication:

For Colleen and Geoffrey

ISBN 0-89747-376-0

If you have any photographs of aircraft, armor, soldiers or ships of any nation, particularly wartime snapshots, why not share them with us and help make Squadron/Signal's books all the more interesting and complete in the future. Any photograph sent to us will be copied and the original returned. The donor will be fully credited for any photos used. Please send them to:

Squadron/Signal Publications, Inc.
1115 Crowley Drive.
Carrollton, TX
USA 75011-5010

Если у вас есть фотографии самолётов, вооружения кораблей любой страны, особенно, снимки времён і поделитесь с нами и помогите сделать новые книг Эскадрон/Сигнал ещё интереснее. Мы переснимем фотографии и вернём оригиналы. Имена приславш будут сопровождать все опубликованные фотограф Пожалуйста, присылайте фотографии по адресу:

Squadron/Signal Publications, Inc.
1115 Crowley Drive.
Carrollton, TX 75011-5010

軍用機、装甲車両、兵士、軍艦などの写真を所持しておられる方はいらっしゃ ものでも結構です。作戦中に撮影されたものが特に良いのです。Squadron/Sig において、このような写真は内容を一層充実し、興味深くすることができます 写真は、複写の後お返しいたします。出版物中に写真を使用した場合は、必ず させて頂きます。お写真は下記にご送付ください。

Squadron/Signal Publications, Inc.
1115 Crowley Drive.
Carrollton, TX 75011-5010

Honorarium

In memory of Jeff Ethell, a Christian family man, writer, and friend, who has contributed greatly to the historical study of aviation. We'll miss him.

In April of 1945 the Twentieth Air Force enlarged tail markings to improve B-29 unit identification. The 500th BG's small "Z-over-a-square" marking is replaced by a "Z" large enough to cover the entire tail. (USAF)

3

Acknowledgements

While human nature resists the idea of a two-volume trilogy, for seventeen years now, **Air Force Colors Volume III** has resisted closure. In a selective version of writer's block, Volume III has stalled while I have sent other books to press. Many friends have incorrectly assumed a rift between author and publisher - if anything, Squadron/Signal has patiently listened to many years of expectant reports that the book was nearing completion. Now, as the last pages of text slide out of my printer, I am amazed that I was actually able to finish.

For all the delay, **AFC III** today is a better book than it could have been in November 1980. For one thing, a home computer allowed the rapid sorting of the thousands of individual aircraft records necessary to decipher organizational markings such as those used by Fifth Air Force and CBI troop carriers. I've also been able to put additional time into research, and many new records have surfaced in Federal archives. But most importantly, scores of veterans and other specialists have shared their materials and the results of researches.

Although a flood damaged many of my correspondence files, I've been able to recover the names of most of those who have assisted on this project. I thank them, and all those whose names do not appear below, for their selfless contributions to this monograph and for their friendship.

Veterans and their reunion organizations have just celebrated the fiftieth anniversary of their victory over the forces of Imperial Japan. Among those who have supported this book are: J. E. Alford, Sr (6th NFS), Carroll R. Anderson (433rd FS), Albert V. Arnold (348th FG), Hal L. Ashby (311th TCS), Richard Birk (15th FG), F. O. Blair (43rd BG), Richard H. Bowen (311th TCS), D. T. Britt (506th FG), Prentiss "Mick" Burkett (73rd BW), William M. Cleveland (11th BG), Dennis G. Cooper (475th FG), Marty R. Copp (374th TCG), Chris Curle (307th BG), Robert L. Ferguson (67th FS), Iwo M. Foxhoven (42nd BG), Glenn Horton (380th BG), James M. Kendall (307th BG), Wilbur K. Kuhn (348th FG), Francis M. Lambert (2nd RS, Photo), Don Lopez (23rd FG), Elbert Major (70th FS), Berge B. Manoogian (868th BS), Robert H. McKinley (348th FG), Eugene J. Millikin (I-C Wing, ATC), Robert E. Moist (1st ACG), Harold & Esther Oyster (319th BG), Dick Powell (80th FG), William Reynolds (49th FG), Pat Rickard (307th BG), Carroll C. Smith (418th NFS), Gordon F. Spence (51st FG), Vince D. Splane (5th BG), Martin Sporn (307th BG), Jan Thies (Hump Pilots Association), Averille M. Thorn (17th RS, Bomb), Clint Ward (44th FS), Ed W. Wolak (51st FG, 440th BFTS), and Charlie T. Zulfer (159th LS, Commando).

Other authors, researchers, modelers, and enthusiasts - many of them also veterans - who have shared their expertise and photos include: David Aiken, Don Alberts, Gerald W. Asher, Steve Birdsall, G. Knox Bishop, Allan G. Blue, Peter M. Bowers, Tom Brewer, Tom Britton, Burl Burlingame, Milton Caniff, Robert L. Cavanagh, Michael J. Claringbould, Robert Cressman, Charles Darby, Don "Bucky" Dawson, David E. Dembeck, Bob Dougwillo, Bruce Doyle, Arthur Eich, Jack M. Elliott, Steve W. Ferguson, Tom Foote, E. F. Furler, Jr., Bill Greenhalgh, Daniel P. Hagedorn, Stanley R. Hague, III, J. S. Hester, Larry Hickey, Frank Hodges, John Horne, Bruce D. Hoy, Ian D. Huntley, Charlie Hyer, Tom Ivie, Frederick A. Johnsen, John W. Lambert, James F. Lansdale, William T. Larkins, Paul Lawrence, Al T. Lloyd, Bob Lomas, James I. Long, Dave Lucabaugh, Alexander MacPherson, Joe Martin, Paul J. McDaniel, Ernest R. McDowell, James P. Mesko, Mike Monaghan, Jack Morris, Stephen A. Muth, Clyde W. Osborn, David W. Ostrowski, Sam & Carol Parker, Larry Potoski, Bob Pukala, Lee Ragan, Ken Robert, Dirk Romito, Kenn C. Rust, Al G. Simmons, Sam Sox, Jr., John Stanaway, Gregory L. Stone, Dwayne Tabatt, Osamu Tagaya, Norman E. Taylor, Charlie Tennant, Geoff Thomas, Warren E. Thompson, Dave Trost, Clyde Vick, Richard Ward, Ross Whistler, Nick Williams, Kenneth D. Wilson, Edward Wolak, and Ted Young. And Jeff Ethell, the man who has unearthed more color photography than Kodak, was consistently generous with his collections.

Within the Department of the Air Force, several organizations and individuals have supported this project. I miss the Secretary of the Air Force's Magazine & Book Branch; while it was in existence, it was my pleasure to work with such fine individuals as Nick P. Apple, Rick P. DuCharme, and Paul K. Kahl. The staff of the Air Force Museum, including Tom Brewer, Wes Henry, Royal D. Frey, Dave Menard (who also shared many images from his own collections), Vivian M. White, and Charles G. Worman, always made my visits there relaxing and profitable. (I have particularly enjoyed their invitations to present some of this material in their lecture series.) The same can be said of the staffs of the Office of Air Force History, both at Maxwell and at Bolling, including George Cully, James N. Eastman, Jr, Jerry Hasselwander, Larry Paszek, and Barry Spink. Other USAF help came from John Cloe (Alaskan Air Command/HO), the wonderful Alice Price (Art and Museum Branch), B. J. Zirkle (90th SMW/HO), and the staff of the old 1361st Audiovisual Squadron. (Research can never be the same without Fern Street!)

Other official help has come from the many offices and employees of the National Archives, USMC Audiovisual Branch, and US Army Audiovisual Branch, and from the DMA's Roy Stanley.

The staff (now my co-workers) at the National Air and Space Museum has always encouraged my independent work on this project. Some have reviewed chapters and provided sounding boards for ideas. While this was never a Ph.D thesis, many have appreciated that not all serious history needs to be scholarly history.

At Squadron/Signal the text, focus, and layout of book have benefitted from the energies of Jerry Campbell, Bruce Culver, Robert C. Stern, and Chuck Harransky. Don Greer has once again produced beautiful color artwork which is both documentary and dramatic.

My daughter Colleen was two years old when work on this volume was started; now she is a fine young woman and gifted artist attending college. Geoff was born a few months before I extended my first deadline; he's now a seventeen-year-old soccer star and high school student with dreams of becoming a veterinarian. On parts of many weekends they've watched their dad work and helped sort layouts, paint insignia, and make sense of the times before any of us were born.

Susan has been hearing about the long-missing Volume III since we met in 1983. As my bride of ten years now, she has encouraged and supported me through the many days of elusive words and ideas. As an artist, her knowledge of pigments has revealed a side of the color story I had not imagined, and I would not have attempted the insignia drawings in pages 44 and 45 without her instruction. Her love of art introduced me to a whole new world; her love of me has made the rest of the world that much better.

And finally, a word of thanks to you, the readers. Through your comments, letters, phone calls, and Christmas cards (Yes, Bu-rid-ju-san! There is a Santa Claus!), you have stimulated my efforts. After these many years, I hope you find this book has been worth your wait.

Arlington, Virginia
March 1997

319th FG ground crewmen apply black stripes to the yellow tails of their P-47Ns on Ie Shima. A VII Air Force group escorting XX Air Force B-29s, the 319th independently developed and applied its new markings under spartan conditions. (USAF)

Introduction

This is a book about Army Air Forces (AAF) aircraft colors and markings. It covers aircraft operating against Imperial Japan, aircraft and units preparing in the US during World War II, and postwar aircraft through the formation of the United States Air Force in late 1947. During the six years covered in these pages the AAF and the Navy exercised independent (though often coordinated) control of manufacturer- and depot-applied aircraft colors. But while Navy aircraft colors exhibited a uniformity consistent with a strong, centralized authority, Army colors and markings could be altered anywhere in the chain of command. Headquarters correspondence files show frequent negotiations with subordinate commands - not a sign of indecision, but a recognition that each local authority was using paint to deal with differing local requirements. Given this dispersed authority, a study of AAF colors and markings becomes inextricably linked to a study of AAF organizations.

In 1940 the War Department began planning contingencies for a US war against Germany, against Japan, or both. Judging Germany the predominant Axis military power, plans called for a strategic defense against Japan – containing the "less-powerful" Japanese while Allied forces defeated Germany. To this end, on the eve of hostilities the AAF was deploying its most modern aircraft to the Philippines. That the Japanese should so quickly overrun those defenses had been inconceivable, and the first six months after Pearl Harbor saw nearly all of the AAF's available forces brought to the Pacific (or, more properly, the "Asiatic-Pacific Theater"). By mid-October 1942 the AAF recorded 816 aircraft lost in combat against Japan - with only 38 lost against Italy and Germany! Even with the addition of accidental losses, the Pacific was drawing a disproportionate share of aircraft and inhibiting US action in Europe.

Only four numbered air forces (the Eighth, Ninth, Twelfth, and Fifteenth) directed the thousands of AAF aircraft in Europe and the Mediterranean. Eight numbered air forces fought the Japanese, a number reflecting geography more than overall strength (in fact, the entire Eleventh Air Force numbered fewer aircraft than a single Eighth Air Force wing). Aircraft in New Guinea and Australia were assigned to the Fifth Air Force (previously known as the Far East Air Force) in February 1942. The Panama Canal and Caribbean were defended by the Sixth Air Force; Japanese attacks there never materialized, though German U-Boats were a continuing problem. In Hawaii the Seventh Air Force (previously Hawaiian Air Force) was designated in February 1942; The Seventh saw combat throughout the Central Pacific, with much of its strength also diverted to other theaters. The US combat forces in the China-Burma-India Theater (CBI) came under the Tenth Air Force, also in February 1942, though General Claire Chennault's China Air Task Force gained independence as the Fourteenth Air Force in March 1943. To defend the Aleutians and Alaska, AAF combat units there were assembled under the Alaskan Air Force, which became the Eleventh Air Force in February 1942. South Pacific units, including

those in the Solomons, became the Thirteenth Air Force in January 1943. And finally, the Twentieth Air Force was formed in 1944 to control the strategic B-29 assault on the Japanese homeland. The actions (and markings) of each of these numbered air forces were also coordinated with the Allies, Navy air, other numbered air forces, and other combat arms through various higher command organizations.

Several other organizations are also important to this book. The First, Second, Third, and Fourth Air Forces were America's domestic combat organizations. Along with their commitment to the defense of America (which then comprised only 48 states), the four domestic air forces trained units and crews for combat in other theaters. First Troop Carrier Command (not a First Air Force component) fulfilled a similar mission for tactical transport crews. Independent of numbered air forces, Flying Training Command (and later Training Command) were responsible for individual flight training. Air Transport Command carried out the AAF's global strategic airlift. Materiel Command issued technical orders and specifications for aircraft colors. And Materiel Command and Proving Ground Command shared responsibility for developing and evaluating color schemes and paints.

Throughout this book, we will refer to the "US Army Air Forces," an organization whose title was always plural; we will also occasionally use the contemporary synonym "Air Force," although this was an unofficial title. For clarity, when referring to more than one subordinate air force, we will use the lower-case term "numbered air forces." We will also follow the contemporary syntax, which required that air force numbers be spelled out or in Roman numerals; for example, "Tenth Air Force" or "X Air Force," but not "10th Air Force." Reporting to each numbered air force were subordinate, numbered commands, organized along functional lines. Combat commands were also designated with Roman numerals, usually (but not always) matching the number of the parent air force; for example, Fifth AF fighters came under V Fighter Command and Seventh Air Force Bombers under VII Bomber Command, while Twentieth Air Force Bombers came under XX and XXI bomber commands. (Non-combat organizations and many joint authorities were organized as named commands - such as Air Transport Command and Eastern Air Command. As an organizational term, "command" would continue to have multiple definitions until 1946.)

The next authorized level of authority was the "division," an organizational level which saw no use in the Pacific and negligible use in the US. Numbered air forces could also group units under "wings." Combat wings were designated with Arabic numerals; for example, the 91st Reconnaissance Wing was assigned to the Fifth AF, while the 315th Bombardment Wing was assigned to XX Bomber Command under the Twentieth AF. (In the pages that follow we will use the term "wing markings" to refer only to markings assigned by a wing; markings painted on aircraft wings will be described by more precise terms.) The group was the next level of command, with each group commanding several squadrons. Squadron leaders could create flights, designating each with a letter (A, B, C, or D). Note that each of these command levels was created as needed, and unnecessary levels could be omitted – squadrons were occasionally assigned directly to AAF Headquarters! And, as stated previously, each level was capable of generating its own organizational markings.

To better distinguish color names from color descriptions, all color names in this book are capitalized. Thus, "dark green" simply describes a green which is dark, while "Dull Dark Green" identifies a color which was matched to Air Force color number 30. The exception is "OD" or "Olive Drab," which we use to refer to any of the official olive drab shades. References to the "OD scheme" identify the standard AAF camouflage, including Neutral Gray under surfaces. Uncamouflaged aircraft are described as "silver," "aluminum," or, simply, "uncamouflaged," rather than by the popular, if misleading, term "natural metal finish." And the term "standard pattern" refers to any camouflage pattern which is identical on each aircraft.

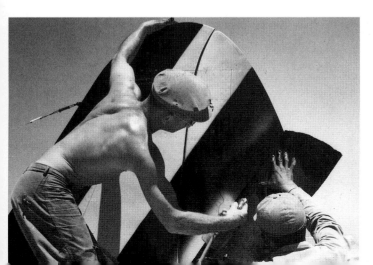

PACIFIC COLORS, 1942-43

CAMOUFLAGE

In 1941 the standard USAAF aircraft camouflage was Dark Olive Drab 41 (or "OD") with Neutral Gray 43 undersides. After April 1941, theater commanders were allowed to substitute greener shades (Medium Green 42 or Sea Green 28) for OD, though there are no indications these substitutions occurred in the Pacific. RAF or Australian greens could also be used, but even forward depots appear to have been well-stocked with USAAF paints. In mid-1943 stocks of Olive Drab (the lighter Army shade which would become ANA color 613) began to replace Dark Olive Drab, but quantities of the older paint remained in use even at the War's end.

Irregular "splotches, patches or stripes" (and patterns varied greatly) of Medium Green 42 were first applied to leading and trailing edges of wings and stabilizers in mid-1942. In theory this lighter color would "... break the continuity of the appearance at the edges." In practice, rapidly fading OD paints usually left the Medium Green edges as a darker border.

For desert operations, Sand 26 ("Desert Pink") was the specified substitute for OD. Although Pacific aircraft were rarely camouflaged for the desert, several Sand-painted 404th BS B-24s were diverted to Alaska in June 1942 - the unit was eventually nicknamed "The Pink Elephants." The 7th BG flew at least one similar Liberator in India.

During 1943, P-39s and P-40s on Canton Island were painted to match the coral sands. The actual color is undocumented, but possibilities include Corps of Engineers color Sand #3 or Desert Sand #10 (the engineers on that treeless island were camouflaging everything in sight!) or AAF Sand 26. Aircraft undersides were painted a light blue of unknown origin.

Haze camouflages [the two reconnaissance schemes first described in AFC II] were applied to many Pacific F-4s, F-5s, and F-7s. Photos from

(Top) Christmas in September! A 12th FS P-39K is repaired beneath the palms of Christmas Island in September 1942. A white ring borders the squadron-colored nose, and the squadron emblem is carried on both cockpit doors. (DIA)

China show Synthetic Haze Paint being field-applied to 40th PRS F-5Es in 1944, ending speculation that the scheme was applied only in the US.

Two unidentified blue paints were used on Pacific B-17s. In June 1942 Lt. Harry Spieth (435th BS, 19th BG) painted the underside of his B-17E a "Sky Blue." The aircraft (41-2421) was lost three weeks later landing at Horn Island. The Hawaiian Air Depot painted one B-17E in an overall blue for over-water patrols. Nicknamed *The Blue Goose*, the aircraft (41-2616) flew with the 11th BG until lost over Shortland Harbor on 29 September 1942. (Crews noted that *The Blue Goose* always drew more than its share of enemy fire.) There are no known photos of either plane.

For night operations, early orders specified Flat Black. Permanent finishes were usually applied overall, as on P-70s, while temporary blacks were generally painted on under surfaces and sides only. The 307th BG B-24Ds which struck Wake Island in December 1942 used a "removable" paint of lamp black and Castile soap; the camouflage left stains which were still visible two years later!

A multi-toned upper-surface camouflage for Pacific B-17s was first mentioned in **Air Force Colors I**. New photos confirm that a standard pattern was used, and that the pigments were permanent. Color images apparently show colors similar to Sea Green 28, Sand 26, and Rust Brown 34 over the original OD/Gray camouflage. While similar B-17s flew with the Fifth, Seventh, and Thirteenth Air Forces, a review of serials reveals that each plane was in Hawaii before April 1942; we tentatively label this camouflage the "HAD (Hawaiian Air Depot) Scheme."

While no Pacific-based B-17s flew in RAF camouflages, British colors were common on variants of the P-39, P-40, and B-24. In some

(Below) *Butchie 2*, a 19th Transport Squadron C-53, delivers Battle of Midway wounded to Hawaii on 8 June 1942. The red centers of the national insignia and the red and white rudder stripes have been overpainted in accordance with Army/Navy directives issued in May. The red/white rudder stripes and two extra wing stars had been applied per a December 1941 Hawaiian Air Force/Navy agreement. (USAF)

cases RAF-bound aircraft were diverted to the AAF, but other AAF aircraft were ordered in RAF colors to speed production. (In fact, instructions for crating Curtiss P-40E-1s specified that insignia decals for the US and RAF be included.) P-40 factory drawings also clarify the camouflage anomalies mentioned in earlier AFC volumes. The "Sand, Medium Green, and pastel blue" colors were company substitutions for RAF Dark Earth, Dark Green, and Sky. Since the British colors were available for other Curtiss products, reasons for the substitutions are obscure. By 1943 most aircraft were being delivered in US colors.

NATIONAL INSIGNIA

In May 1942, the red center was ordered eliminated from the old star insignia to lessen confusion with the Japanese "meatball" insignia. (Field organizations probably initiated the change in March 1942.) In late June 1943, the national insignia changed again, with a white bar added to each side and a red border surrounding the whole. The Fifth and Thirteenth Air Force commanders rejected this marking and, by July, notified Navy counterparts that the red border would not be applied; on 2 August Washington was notified. Following a series of cables, the Chief of Air Staff agreed to standardize the Pacific version of the insignia - a white star tangent to a blue circle with white side bars and no surround! Pacific commanders would be satisfied, man-hours needed to paint the insignia would be reduced, and number of necessary paints would be cut from three to two. (Following a brief discussion of green borders, a blue surround was suggested if contrast was needed between the white bars and light backgrounds.) But by the time overseas commands were notified on 30 August, Materiel Command and the Navy had already revised the insignia: on 14 August they agreed that the border would be retained using Insignia Blue. The unbordered insignia never made the tech orders, but could be found on Pacific aircraft through the end of the war.

THEATER MARKINGS

Camouflage might make aircraft less visible, but identification of friendly forces was often more critical. Confusion over the South and Southwest Pacific was lessened somewhat by the use of white fighter ID markings. The first of these appeared in March or April 1943, when the Thirteenth Air Force and Royal New Zealand Air Force applied white wing, tail, and fuselage stripes to their P-40s on Guadalcanal. Orders explaining the origins of these markings have, so far, proved elusive.

It is also unclear how the tails of SOPAC/SWPA fighters first came to be painted white. Though the marking is often traced to a September 1943 Fifth Air Force memo, this document was issued long after the paint had dried. A 24 July photo shows the markings on an early Fifth AF P-47. The marking was also photographed on Thirteenth AF P-40s at Guadalcanal in July and at Munda on 13 August. As early as June, the Fifth and Thirteenth air force commanders had conferred on friendly fighter markings, acknowledging instances of confusion between Japanese and Allied fighters; either may have initiated the white tail

TWIN NIFTY'S was a B-24D of the Fifth Air Force's 90th BG. As the area's only B-24 group in late 1942, the 90th had no need of elaborate unit markings. Individual nose art and mission scores were repeated on both sides of each 90th Liberator. (90th BMW)

marking, or they may have planned the marking together. September 27th photos show Fifth AF P-47s with white tails and wing leading edges; it was this combination which was standardized for Fifth AF and RAAF single-engined fighters, though white leading edges were often later deleted, and many units later restricted the tail markings to vertical surfaces only. Thirteenth AF and RNZAF P-40s continued to carry their white wing and fuselage bands, with the addition of all-white tails. Marine and Navy aircraft in theater, and Thirteenth AF P-39s made no use of the markings.

UNIT MARKINGS

A segment of color on the tail or nose often identified a squadron within a group, and unit insignia were often proudly displayed - the AAF never outlawed these emblems. Tech orders also carried the prewar system of group, squadron, and flight leader stripes until June 1943, when authority for command markings was left to theater commanders.

The markings of individual Pacific units are poorly documented, due both to the lack of surviving records and photos and the heavy trading of airframes between units. Squadrons of the 8th and 35th fighter groups, for example, switched bases and P-39s on several occasions; as it was often easier to move crews and commands than to move aircraft, unit colors and aircraft ID numbers quickly lost their original meanings.

The most common individual aircraft marking during the first two years of the Pacific war was the plane-in-unit number. Squadrons could number (or letter) their aircraft, or groups could assign number ranges to each squadron. At various times, commands in the V, VII, and XIII air forces assigned unique number ranges to each squadron; atypically, the Fourteenth Air Force assigned distinguishing number ranges to all of its squadrons. These systems were periodically realigned to reflect changing unit assignments and tracing all of the ranges has not been possible. The 49th FG's 9th FS, for example, carried tail numbers in the 200s and 300s during February 1942; by June the same airframes sported numbers between 70 and 99, with blocks of ten assigned to each flight. Surviving VII FC documents (see page 11) indicate the scope of these number systems. (Note also that the Seventh's fuselage stripes were altered to accommodate both the larger mid-1943 national insignia and frequent unit reassignments.)

Aircraft could be shared as well as traded. In December 1942, while the 44th FS waited to move its P-40s to Guadalcanal, 44th pilots flew P-39 missions with the 67th FS. The 67th was assigning aircraft numbers between 2 and 61 at that time, and aircraft 51 to 56 were reserved for 44th's crews. Shortages of fighters on Guadalcanal in 1943 forced the 18th FG to pool the pilots and aircraft of its 12th FS with the 347th FG's 67th and 68th Squadrons. Together they flew P-39s, P-400s, and P-40s marked for whoever had last applied paint. Later in 1943, 70th FS P-38s were flown by pilots of both groups, while the 70th flew some of its missions in P-39s. A similar shortage of B-17s led to a pooling between the 5th and 11th bomb groups.

As will be seen, the markings of Pacific units became more elaborate on silver aircraft as combat formations grew in size and as forward bases became less vulnerable to enemy attack.

(Above) Using American paints, a 51st FG P-40K wears the RAF Temperate Scheme of Dark Earth and Dark Green over Sky under surfaces. On Tenth AF aircraft a plane-in-group number replaces the radio call number; a 51st FG shark mouth has been painted on the nose. The "Tom Collins" rudder emblem is a personal marking. March 1943. (USAF)

(Below) A 343rd FG P-40K, in the RAF Temperate Scheme, taxies out for an early 1943 Aleutian patrol. The yellow spinner front was common on 18th FS Warhawks. (USAF)

(Above) Curtiss painters use rubber templates to camouflage a set of P-40 wings. RAF or US national insignia decals could be applied at the factory or shipped with the crated airframe for application on delivery. (AFM)

(Below) A 49th FG P-40E over Australia in 1943. White bars flank the fuselage star, which also has a darker ring around the original cockade. The fin and spinner appear to be in a squadron color or Olive Drab. (Moran via Mesko)

(Above) Bell stocks of Dark Earth, Dark Green, and Sky were fairly compatible with RAF specs. This P-400 (s/n BW134) carries the shark mouth and light-gray spinner of the 80th FS. The 8th FG's aircraft letter replaces the tail number "37" applied when this aircraft flew with the 35th FG. (Moran via Mesko)

(Below) It was the 8th Photo Reconnaissance Squadron that first took the Lockheed F-4 into combat. This F-4A has zinc oxide sprayed over a black base coat resulting in a graded blue scheme known as Haze Paint. The spinners carry red, white, and blue rings. (Moran via Mesko)

(Above) A P-400 assigned to the 67th FS on Guadalcanal. The unit markings include white wing tips and a distinctive shark mouth. (USMC via Ward)

(Below) B-24Ds of the 307th BG on Midway prior to the December 1942 strike on Wake. The night raid marked the anniversary of Wake's falling to the Japanese, and was the Seventh AF's first heavy bomber mission. A "temporary" finish of lamp black and castile soap covers the under surface and sides. (USAF)

(Above) At least ten B-17Es were repainted at the Hawaiian Air Depot in 1941/42. Seen on New Caledonia this B-17 carries a standard pattern of what appears to be Sea Green, Rust Brown, and Sand over the factory finish of Olive Drab and Neutral Gray. (USAF)

(Below) The left side of *Old Maid*, which crashed on Guadalcanal in November 1942. Col. Walter Sweeney had flown the same aircraft at the Battle of Midway five months earlier. (National Archives)

(Above) A Fifth Air Force B-17E shows an identical pattern sprayed over the original Olive Drab. Note the remotely operated belly turret. (The same aircraft appears on page 85 of AIR FORCE COLORS VOL. I.) (Lloyd)

(Below) The Hawaiian Air Depot developed a similar multicolor pattern for its B-18s. Serial 37-002 crashed at Hickam in May 1943. (USAF)

VII FIGHTER COMMAND OPERATIONS MEMO #21
IDENTIFICATION MARKINGS OF AIRCRAFT, 20 July 1943

1. For the purpose of identification of airplanes assigned to organizations of this command, colors and blocks of numbers are assigned as follows:

Organization	Color	Numbers
HQ VII FC		1-14
CO, 15th Fighter Gp		15
6th Night Fighter Sq	Blue (dark)	16-49
45th Fighter Squadron	Green (light)	50-99
46th Fighter Squadron	White	100-149
47th Fighter Squadron	Blue (robin egg)	150-199
78th Fighter Squadron	Yellow	200-249
CO 318th Fighter Gp		300
19th Fighter Squadron	Blue (robin egg)	301-349
72d Fighter Squadron	Yellow	350-399
73d Fighter Squadron	White	400-449
333d Fighter Squadron	Green (light)	450-499

2. The numerals, approximately twenty inches high and twelve inches wide with a two-and-one-half-inch stroke, will be painted on with white calamine. They will be located on the cowling of the P-40 type aircraft, centered immediately beneath the exhaust stacks. On the P-39s they will be just forward of the cockpit door and will lie along the horizontal axis of the plane.

3. Group Markings will be as follows:

a. The 15th Fighter Group marking will consist of two painted bands five inches in width encircling cowling. The first band will be just forward of the coolant cowl flap and the other band just aft of the entering edge of the coolant radiator cowling aperture. (The numerals will be located between the two.)

b. The 318th Fighter Group marking will be a single band five inches in width encircling cowling just forward of coolant cowl flap.

c. On P-39s, in both the 15th and 318th Fighter Groups, the band encircling the cowling will be just forward of the leading edge of the the wing.

Shelbe IV wears its two 15th FG nose bands in yellow, the 78th FS squadron color. The P-40K carries its radio call number (246104) on the rudder only. (USAF)

The 44th FS moved from Hawaii to the New Hebrides in late 1942. Seventh Air Force markings — extra wing insignia, an 18th FG fuselage band, and 44th FS horizontal white bar - are still evident as this P-40F is barged to shore. (National Archives)

VII Fighter Command Group Stripes

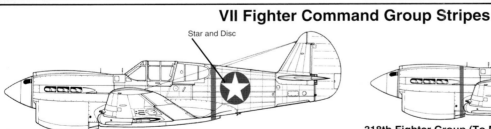

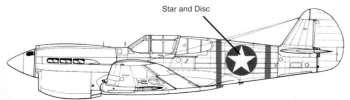

Star and Disc

18th Fighter Group (to early 1943)
318th Fighter Group (From Mid 1944)

Star and Disc

15th Fighter Group (To Mid 1943)

Barred Insignia

318th Fighter Group (To Mid 1944)
21st Fighter Group (From Mid 1944)

Barred Insignia

15th Fighter Group (From Mid 1943)

(Above) *Black Magic* has the blue tail tip of the 348th FG's 342nd FS. White bars to the national insignia were masked with tape, leaving white over spray "ghosts"; the insignia are unbordered. Note how the factory number "280" (near the fuselage star) and serial (42-8132) correlate with those on the aircraft at the bottom of this page (287 and 42-8139). (Delong via Mesko)

(Below) *Destitute Prostitute*, a 44th FS P-40F on Munda in August 1943, has the white tail carried by most Allied fighters in the South and Southwest Pacific areas. The dark "borders" of the original Thirteenth Air Force stripes resulted from white overspray of masking tape. The fuselage insignia is a simple white star on blue disc. (National Archives)

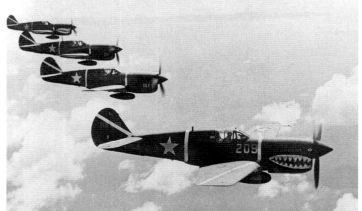

(Above)These 68th and 44th FS P-40Fs display the radiating wing and tail stripes carried by Thirteenth AF and RNZAF Warhawks stationed in the South Pacific. April 1943. (National Archives)

(Below) An early P-47D over Australia in mid-1943. Fifth AF painters generally masked the tail number, leaving an OD background on an all-white tail. Unit markings and white leading edges are not yet applied, and the national insignia is unmodified. (Moran via Mesko)

National Insignia

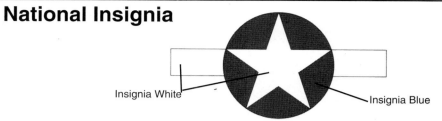

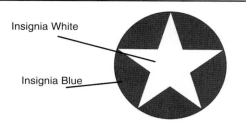

May 1944

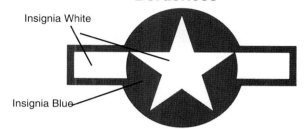

July 1943 (Fifth AF Variation)

Borderless

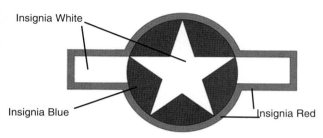

June 1943 (AN-I- 9a)

August 1943 (AN-I-96)

(Below) *El Diablo IV*, a B-25D of the 345th BG's 499th BS, banks over Borgen Bay the day after Christmas 1943. National insignia are unbordered, and the white bars are centered on the discs, not meeting the points of the stars. (USAF)

(Below) A P-47D of the 8th FG's 36th FS at Port Moresby in December 1943. White wing leading edges had been adopted by the Fifth AF the previous September. The aircraft letters and the white nose ring were originally carried by the 36th's P-39s. (via Lucabaugh)

(Below) By early 1944 the 36th FS traded its squadron letters for numbers. Numbers were also briefly carried on the 36th's P-38s before the squadron returned to aircraft letters. Nadzab, New Guinea. (Steffanic via Tagaya)

(Above) Another 15th FG squadron, the 46th, carried the rarely seen coral and blue camouflage from March through December of 1943. *Devastating Devil* was a P-39Q photographed shortly before the unit moved to Makin Island where the aircraft were repainted Olive Drab and Neutral Gray. (Garnett via Lambert)

(Below) Stenciled information was often masked off during the repainting, leaving strips of OD or Neutral Gray after removal of the tape. (USAF)

(Above) The 15th FG's 45th FS moved its P-40Ns to the coral Phoenix Islands in September 1943. On arrival at Canton Island, the Warhawks were repainted a coral sand color with pale blue under surface. Note the red surrounds to the national insignia. (USAF)

(Below) The SWPA modification of B-25s as strafers encouraged the addition of various fearsome paint jobs. This black and white skull was used by the 3rd BG's 13th BS during mid-June 1943. (US Army)

HIGHER VISIBILITY

In late 1942 air force policy offices began to debate the merits of standard camouflage, unpainted metal, and smoothed (polished) camouflage. Improvements in speed, manufacturing costs, and surface maintenance hours were contrasted with increases in visibility and corrosion; unpainted metal appeared to offer major advantages in the first three categories, with minor disadvantages in the latter two. In March 1943 the eleven numbered air forces were brought into the debate in a memo which touted a 20- to 25-mile-per-hour speed increase on uncamouflaged aircraft (a figure inflated by improperly calibrated tests) and which questioned their requirements for aircraft camouflage. The Fourteenth Air Force insisted on retaining camouflage; their own tests on several stripped P-40s found a speed increase of only 5 MPH - not considered much of an advantage while the enemy was still close enough to strike at forward bases. The Eleventh and Sixth air forces and the Western Defense Command favored abandonment of camouflage. The Seventh Air Force requested only a sky-blending under surface; ground camouflage could be applied locally if needed. The Thirteenth, unconcerned with daytime camouflage, asked that aluminum skins be dulled to a neutral shade and requested a "non-reflecting" black paint for night bombing. Although the Fifth Air Force's General Kenney required camouflage for his aircraft, it was Kenney who first sent unpainted AAF aircraft into combat. The 22nd BG had begun B-25 transition in January 1943, but enough B-26s were rebuilt and stripped

to equip one squadron; these 19th BS Marauders, soon known as "The Silver Fleet," returned to combat in New Guinea in June 1943.

In October 1943 Washington finally revised its policy and deleted the requirement for factory-applied camouflage on most Army Air Forces aircraft. But the policy change did not bring an end to camouflage - it simply ended the requirement for camouflage on most new production - and some existing contracts continued to deliver camouflaged aircraft through mid-1944. Transports, night fighters, recon aircraft, and liaison types were exempted from the new policy, and theater commanders could always paint any aircraft if they wished.

The requirements for stripping camouflage from aircraft and components showed similar flexibility. Only B-29s and P-38s were ordered stripped at the factory; factories were otherwise free to deliver aircraft camouflaged, uncamouflaged, or with a patchwork of camouflaged and uncamouflaged components. Theater commanders also had options to strip their aircraft.

Pacific commanders became interested in the 1943 development of Jet Black paint (ANA 622) first created for P-61 night fighters. By

Marauders of the 22nd BG's 19th BS on a 1943 mission. The white bars of the unbordered national insignia contrast poorly with the aluminum fuselages, while the simpler star-and-disc serves as the wing insignia of the nearest B-26. Barely visible on the third aircraft is the *Silver Fleet* rudder emblem. (Roy Parker via AFM)

February 1944 the Fifth, Eleventh, Thirteenth, and Fourteenth air forces had ordered enough of the "anti-searchlight paint" to camouflage almost three hundred B-24s, B-25s, and P-38s. The paint was shipped, but with few aircraft dedicated to night missions the glossy black finish saw limited use. Jet Black was most prevalent in the two Snooper squadrons of the Fifth and Thirteenth air forces, on B-24s of the Tenth and Fourteenth air forces, and eventually on the Twentieth Air Force's B-29s.

As the use of camouflage declined, the use of special identification markings increased. On 9 October 1944 Thirteenth Air Force bombers preparing for a joint mission to Balikpapan were notified that the Fifth Air Force P-47 fighter cover would be marked with a single thirty-inch black stripe around each wing and a similar stripe around the aft fuselage. Variations of these markings were eventually carried by all Fifth Air Force P-47s and P-51s, although the number of bands in each position could vary from one to four - even on the same aircraft! Photos (but no documents) from March 1944 also record the Fifth's propensity to carry prewar-style red/white/blue rudder stripes on both bombers and fighters.

In the CBI the Tenth Air Force began marking its P-38s, P-47s, and P-51s with white or Insignia Blue (or black) stripes in late 1944. One stripe was painted around each wing, one stripe around each vertical and horizontal tail plane, and one at the cowl front or spinner. (The British adopted the markings in mid-January 1945; as stipulated by the joint US/UK Eastern Air Command, the markings became known as EAC Stripes.) In February 1945 orders were modified to keep the stripes from covering ailerons, elevators, or rudders. The only Fourteenth Air Force unit to carry a version of the markings was the 81st FG, which added the wing stripes and its own fuselage stripe, but usually omitting the tail stripes.

Unit aircraft markings could be specified by air force commands, but

Fighters in the Philippines - Mustangs and Thunderbolts show off their markings. Two 110th TRS F-6s carry six wing stripes; three more of the squadron's aircraft have four each, and one is unmarked. The white-tailed 35th FG P-47 has five wing stripes, while across the mat its squadron mate has only one, which is white on a camouflaged wing! Fuselage stripes show a similar lack of uniformity. (USAF)

Thar She Blows, an 11th Bomb Group B-24, shows the Neutral Gray paint added as sky camouflage. Stars over the bomb mission symbols were authorized by the Seventh AF in 1942 to designate outstanding missions. Guam, May 1945. (USAF)

most Pacific groups and squadrons developed their own. The Thirteenth Air Force's Crusaders (42nd BG) and the Fifth Air Force's Jolly Rogers (90th BG), for example, designed markings appropriate to their nicknames. While some group markings made squadrons more recognizable at a distance or expressed a certain esprit de corps, squadron markings were not always necessary: the 41st BG, for example, saw eight months of combat before any of its squadrons flew together on a mission. But the story of the 433rd Fighter Squadron's markings is a classic.

As related by the late Carroll R. Anderson, the 433rd FS had a certain maverick aspect, one he described as an "attitude of independence." Taking advantage of group commander Charles MacDonald's stateside leave, the 433rd started giving their P-38s a truly unique color scheme. The wing tips were to be blue with white piping, as would the tops and bottoms of the vertical tails. Radiator intakes, prop spinners, nose and engine antiglare panels, and plane-in-group numbers would be solid blue; each wing would have a white-bordered diagonal blue band, with white accent stripes on wing leading edges.

Painting proved difficult: high temperatures and low humidities dried the blue dope almost as fast as it was brushed onto the aircraft. Dope thinner ran out, as did blue dope and masking tape (cheat stripes had to be applied by hand). On any given day, seventeen of the P-38s could be flying long missions and unavailable for painting. And there was a time element: MacDonald's leave was to last for only thirty days! Anderson, his crew chief, and the squadron painter finished repainting Anderson's P-38 *Virginia Marie* with a few days to spare.

On his return, MacDonald ordered all painting stopped immediately. Only *Virginia Marie* was finished, and the rest of the squadron's aircraft were left in rather motley condition. As punishment for the unauthorized paint job, squadron members were required to polish an aluminum ring on each spinner. Soon afterward, many 475th FG P-38s (including *Virginia Marie*) were transferred to the 49th FG replacing heavy losses at Tacloban. The 433rd's miss-marked aircraft were gone forever, and the squadron returned to its simple plane-in-group numbers and blue tail tips.

Such diversity in marking systems defies a single listing. Page 18 will briefly review the colors of the Homefront and Air Transport Command. The following three chapters will deal with the Pacific markings of every individual USAAF unit. Fighters, bombers, transports, and other types will be grouped under three headings: Pacific Basin (Fifth, Seventh, Eleventh, and Thirteenth air forces) starting on page 24; China-Burma-India (Tenth and Fourteenth air forces and ATC units) starting on page 58; and the USAAF's strategic B-29 assault against Japan (Twentieth Air Force) from page 83.

(Above)*VIRGINIA MARIE*, Carroll Anderson's P-38J, bakes in the Biak sun with the completed 433rd FS "independent" paint scheme, including the mandated aluminum spinner stripe. (Anderson)

(Below) Field-applied camouflage: paint is sprayed on the unprimed skin of a 42nd BG B-25H. (USAF)

(Above)Spinners stripped with steel wool, crew chief Sgt. Joseph Poplowski marks a line where he will reapply blue dope on the spinner front. The name on the right nose is *MARGARET.* (Anderson)

(Below) *Carlotta,* an 80th FG P-47D in India, 1944. The white Tenth Air Force stripes are 28-inches wide on the wings, and 18-inches wide on the tail. The first 17 inches of the cowl are also white, in this case representing the 88th FS squadron color. (Peter M. Bowers)

17

THE HOME FRONT

Markings on "The Home Front" appear to show a random confusion of aircraft numbers, with the occasional odd color combination. These colors and markings were created by several organizations, including HQ USAAF, Training Command, four numbered air forces, several schools and test organizations, and Air Transport Command.

Reporting directly to USAAF Headquarters, Flying Training Command (FTC) was established in February 1942 to supervise the Southeast, Gulf Coast, and West Coast Army Air Forces Training Centers. These three centers instructed individuals in flying skills and the essentials of military life. In July 1943 Flying Training Command merged with Technical Training Command (which trained ground crews and mechanics) to form Training Command (TC). The three air training centers were concurrently reorganized as subordinate commands: Eastern, Central, and Western flying training commands.

Prospective pilots faced primary, basic, and advanced flight schools: If graduated, these aviators would still need instruction in an operational aircraft and in the techniques of flying and fighting as part of a unit. Pilots who were transitioning to heavy and medium bombers first went to the appropriate Training Command schools, then to a numbered air

A green-cowled AT-6B from Spense Field, Georgia, in mid-1944. In April Materiel Command approved removal of the fuselage insignia to make room for field numbers on the aft fuselage; this Texan has not yet been repainted. (Wolak)

force unit for unit/crew training. Pilots learning other aircraft moved directly to units under Air Transport Command, First Troop Carrier Command (TCC), or one of the numbered air forces.

In addition to combat responsibilities, each domestic numbered air force had a primary (not exclusive) training responsibility. The First Air Force (in what was roughly the north-east quarter of the US) and Fourth Air Force (south-west quarter) trained and organized fighter groups; the Second Air Force (north-west quarter) was the center of heavy bomber and very-heavy bomber training; and the Third Air Force (south-east quarter) concentrated on light and medium bombers. The First Troop Carrier Command (not a geographic organization) trained all troop carrier (tactical transport) crews and units.

Domestic combat groups were generally Operational Training Units (OTUs) or Replacement Training Units (RTUs). Once declared operational, an OTU could be sent overseas for combat, while RTUs trained aircrews for operations with other units. By 1944 virtually all USAAF combat units (excluding the B-29 groups) had been formed, and RTUs predominated. In May 1944, remaining RTUs were merged with air base units to form combat crew training schools, and most of the associated combat groups were inactivated.

In October 1940 the Army had specified that camouflaged aircraft would carry one star insignia above the left wing, one below the right wing, and one on either side of the aft fuselage, and no rudder stripes. For uncamouflaged aircraft (which included most trainers) different orders applied. Rudder stripes were eliminated in June 1942. The two-position wing stars were specified in November 1942, although there was no order to remove existing insignia from above the right wing and below the left wing. Addition of the fuselage insignia was first ordered in August 1942, but Headquarters had not taken into account the large field numbers painted on the fuselages most FTC aircraft. FTC considered the field numbers an important tool for tracking and evaluating the progress of individual trainees; the "new" fuselage insignia meant field numbers would be smaller or in a less visible position. The policy was subjected to several years of debate until April 1944, when Material Command allowed Training Command to remove the fuselage stars as necessary.

The Insignia Blue "U.S. ARMY" marking under the wings of camouflaged aircraft had been dropped in July 1942. The same marking, painted Black on uncamouflaged aircraft, was no longer required after November 1942 and ordered removed in December 1943.

FTC/TC field numbers were rarely based on the aircraft serial number. Each base would designate flights or squadrons with a range of numbers (and often a color). The three flying training centers/commands independently selected code letters for each field; for example, an "S" field

---

SOUTHEAST ARMY AIR FORCES TRAINING CENTER
AIRCRAFT MARKINGS - 20 MAY 1942

Primary - Primary airplanes will be identified by a number only. Numbers run from 1 to 999 at the discretion of the detachment commander.

Basic and Advanced - [Mark with a] code group consisting of an identifying letter or letters ... plus a digit or digits from 1 to 999. ... The letter number combination will be consecutive with no dash or space inserted between.

Augusta - A	Moody - MO
Cochran - C	Napier - N
Columbus - CO	Shaw - S
Craig - CR	Spense - SP
Eglin - E	Turner - T
Greenville - GR	Tuskegee - TU
Gunter - G	Tyndall - TY
Maxwell - M	

Four-Engine Schools - Four-Engine Schools will not use an identifying letter but will use an identifying number of not more than two digits.

(Above) B-17Gs from Rapid City, South Dakota, practice formation without fear of Flak or enemy fighters. Rapid City was a replacement training unit (RTU); these crews would eventually be dispersed as replacements among existing Eighth and Fifteenth Air Force B-17 units. (USAF)

(Below) An A-26B over South Carolina. The field codes on the nose can be deciphered as "F" for Florence Field, "Y" as the individual aircraft identification letter, and "1" as the first squadron. The Anti-glare panels are Olive Drab. (USAF)

(Above) Looking a little worse for wear, this P-47C flew air defense and training missions out of Norfolk, Virginia, in early 1945. Two guns have been removed from the left wing. (Britt)

number prefix on a West Coast trainer designated Marana, Arizona; in the Southeast it meant Shaw, South Carolina.

The numbered air forces developed their own field markings. First and Fourth air force markings were similar to training markings. Second Air Force painted two-letter tail codes on its heavy bombers; field numbers could draw from the serial or be devised by the field. Third Air Force developed a three-character designator for its medium and light bombers, with the first letter for the field, the last digit for the squadron, and the middle letter for the individual aircraft. The last two characters were generally repeated on tails.

Fabric failure caused by yellow dope had forced a 1941 decision standardizing aluminum finish for all trainers. In March 1944 Training Command recommended that primary trainers again be finished in blue and yellow to improve visibility and safety. After some discussion, in August tech orders authorized PTs to carry a thirty-inch International Orange fuselage band and International Orange wing tips. In July 1945 this was revised to authorize Orange Yellow above the top wing, below the bottom wing, and on all tail surfaces. Basic and advanced trainer schemes were unchanged.

Several other schemes were devised for specific missions. Instrument trainers began carrying Insignia Red vertical tails and ring cowls (and noses for multi-engined aircraft) and an Insignia Red, eighteen-inch diagonal stripe above and below each wing. Fighters used as targets for movie camera gunnery training were marked with bold white stripes on fuselages and wings. Frangible bullet training RP-63 Kingcobras were painted overall International Orange. Radio-controlled targets, such as the Culver PQ-14, were overall Insignia Red with wing leading edges in Orange Yellow. (The Orange Yellow was dropped from specs by March 1944.) Tow target tugs began to wear Orange Yellow rudders, cowlings, and wing tips in August 1943. And after the war, Training Command helicopters were painted overall International Orange, while rescue helicopters wore overall Orange Yellow.

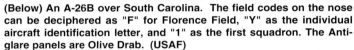

SECOND AND THIRD AIR FORCE CODES

Second Air Force

AR - Harvard, NE
DY - Dyersburg, TN
FA - Fairmont, NE
PY - Pyote, TX
RC - Rapid City, SD

Third Air Force

B (letter-#) Barksdale, LA
F (letter-#) Florence, SC
G (letter-#) Greenville, SC
J (letter-#) Jackson, MS
L (letter-#) Lake Charles, LA

(Above) This PT-17 has the International Orange fuselage band and wing tips authorized for primary trainers between August 1944 and July 1945. Because radio call numbers made little sense on aircraft without radios, in December 1943 Training Command received permission to omit the radio calls from its primary trainers. (Larkins)

(Below) A blue-cowled, silver BT-13A (41-22106) at Cochran Field in October 1943. Orders requiring the removal of the under wing "U.S. ARMY" markings would be published in December. (Wolak)

(Above) A PT-27 from Blythe, California, displays the post-July 1945 primary trainer colors: Identification Yellow on all tail surfaces, above the top wing, and below the lower wing. The dark rectangle beneath the aft cockpit is an Insignia Red fire extinguisher panel. (Bowers)

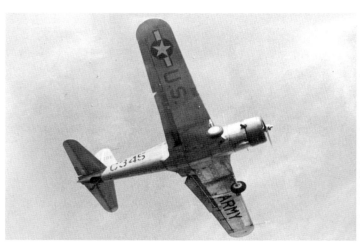

(Below) An AT-6C instrument trainer, photographed in January 1946. The vertical tail, cowl, and diagonal wing stripes are Insignia Red; the radio call number (284491) is Identification Yellow. The post-war "Buzz Number" is described on page 90. (Bowers)

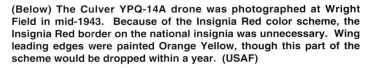

(Above) An AT-6C from Laredo, Texas, complies with Materiel Command policy in May 1943. The national insignia on the aft fuselage forces the field number forward, over the wing. The complete radio call number is painted on the aft fuselage; the application of the last four digits to the fin is unusual. The anti-glare panel is Bronze Green. (USAF)

(Below) The Culver YPQ-14A drone was photographed at Wright Field in mid-1943. Because of the Insignia Red color scheme, the Insignia Red border on the national insignia was unnecessary. Wing leading edges were painted Orange Yellow, though this part of the scheme would be dropped within a year. (USAF)

(Above) International Orange RP-63As from Laredo Field, Texas: the bright color scheme gave gunnery students a better target. Gunners also knew that any aircraft painted another color would be far more vulnerable than the heavily armored RP-63s. (USAF)

(Below) A post-war photo of an RA-25A target tug. Rudder, cowl, and wing tips were the standard Identification Yellow; the fuselage band of the same color was a common addition. The aircraft had served with the 445th FS at Bakersfield, California. (Larkins)

AIR TRANSPORT COMMAND

In July 1942 the Air Transport Command (ATC) was developed from Ferrying Command (activated May 1941) to provide worldwide airlift of cargo and personnel. The new command was independent of the numbered air forces, which were expected to provide their own local airlift through assigned troop carrier units. ATC's Ferrying Division shipped aircraft between stations, units, depots and factories, while the Air Transport Division transported cargoes. ATC also organized nine overseas wings to maintain base facilities, to service transports, and to brief transient crews. Aircraft were usually not assigned to these wings, though requirements for regularly scheduled missions occasionally mandated such assignments. The India-China Wing was the most notable exception, requiring hundreds of aircraft and pilots to resupply China over the Hump (see page 64). ATC was also responsible for the transition training of its own aircrews through six operational training units. Ferrying Division operated the Military Air Transport Service for moving personnel between stations in the US. (This "MATS" should not be confused with the Military Air Transport Service formed by the merger of the ATC and the Naval Air Transport Service in June 1948.)

For markings, ATC aircraft invariably displayed the command insignia on their aft fuselages. The emblem had evolved from the Ferrying Command insignia, substituting a silver background for the gold one and changing the Morse-encoded border letters to "A-F-A-T-C" from "A-F-F-C". In 1942 the Domestic Transport

Early standard markings for the Domestic Transport Division comprised a yellow nose, wing tips, and fuselage band. (Note the dangerous, unintentional similarities to the target tug markings on the previous page!) The ATC emblem would be within the band on the plane's left side. The red cowl stripe and yellow "25" (repeated on the nose in black) may reflect use by an OTU. (USAF)

Division was granted permission to mark its aircraft with Orange-Yellow noses, wing tips, and fuselage bands. Individual ATC aircraft used the last three or four digits of the serial on their tails, and often inside a white or yellow lozenge on the nose. A horizontal yellow band began to appear on vertical tails late in the war.

Many aircraft assigned to the Alaskan Division wore Insignia Red tails and wing upper surfaces, this for higher visibility in the event of forced landings. The wing colors eventually evolved into upper and lower surfaces of the wing tips only.

Ferrying Division's Military Air Transport Service developed its own insignia, carried on the noses of C-47s and C-54s. Service with Military Air Evacuation (MAE) squadrons could be noted with the words "Air Evacuation" or the letters "MAE".

After the war, many Atlantic Division C-54s were marked with airline-style fuselage-length, black-trimmed, red flashes, while the Pacific Division used markings in blue with gold accents.

This ATC C-54D was outfitted for medical evacuation. The nose marking is red with black borders with the Continental Division's Military Air Evacuation emblem. 1946. (USAF)

Captain Paul L. Hexter (center) supervises the application of his first "confusion camouflage" at Eglin. The white areas of this P-51A were masked with paper and tape prior to application of the black. Upper surfaces remained Olive Drab. A recon camera window has been fitted behind the cockpit. (USAF)

CAMOUFLAGE TESTS

While shadow shading, haze paint, and anti-submarine camouflages had their experimental phases before operational use, other camouflage experiments, often successful, never saw service. The best known of these was a "confusion camouflage" tested by the AAF Proving Ground Command at Eglin Field in mid-1943. The sides and under surfaces of a P-51A were repainted with a black and white disruptive pattern in an effort to divert attention to focal points away from the aircraft, disrupt perception, and make the aircraft appear smaller. The scheme, however, proved ineffective in flight tests.

During those tests several combat pilots recommended repainting a P-51 to resemble a P-40. A light blue paint (four parts Insignia White to one part Insignia Blue) was sprayed around the square edges of wing tips and tail planes. To improve contrast, Insignia White was feathered just inside the blue. Then, using a template to produce a hard edge, flat black was vignetted into the Olive Drab (or Neutral Gray on undersides). The 20mm wing cannons were painted with the light blue mix. In tests the deception worked - unless silhouetted, the Mustang was easily mistaken for a P-40. Project engineers hoped that Allied gunners would no longer confuse the P-51 with the Me 109, and that enemy fighters, uncertain of their opponents, would be forced to modify their tactics, but the scheme was never adopted.

Another Eglin disruptive scheme saw a B-24D repainted with false canopies, engines, and flying surfaces. Test reports have not yet been surfaced, though the scheme was later parodied on a 392nd BG B-24D formation ship in England.

(Below) The second "confusion camouflage" rounded the wing and stabilizer tips of a P-51. Seen against the hard stand, the scheme is less than effective. Shadows further betray this Mustang's identity. (NARA)

(Below) A side view of the same aircraft (41-37325) shows how much more effective the scheme was when viewed against the sky. (NARA)

(Below) Eglin's B-24D "confusion camouflage" was tested on 42-40196. Reports of this test have not yet surfaced. (Bowers)

UNIT MARKINGS OF THE PACIFIC BASIN

Alaskan air defense and bombing missions against the Japanese Kuriles were handled by the Eleventh AF. The Eleventh, which never controlled more than five combat groups, never required an air force or command level system of aircraft markings. A span-wise white stripe on the horizontal tails of XI AF and Navy single-engined aircraft was briefly employed as a theater marking but the origin of this marking is unclear.

In the Central Pacific, the Seventh AF began marking fighters with plane-in-command numbers in late 1941, adding group fuselage stripes early in 1942. (The system was discontinued by mid-1944.) The Seventh's heavy bombers began using geometric tail markings in early 1944.

Fifth Air Force fighter groups based in Australia briefly used a system of plane-in-command numbers: 8th FG with 1-99, 35th FG with 100-199, and 49th FG with 200-299. By June 1942 the fighters used plane-in-group numbers or RAAF styled individual aircraft letters. Most later Fifth AF unit markings originated at group level, with troop carrier numbers assigned by the wings.

Guadalcanal drew several Fifth and Seventh air force units to the South Pacific in mid-1942; these units became the Thirteenth Air Force in January 1943. The Thirteenth's fighters appear to have used a plane-in-command numbering system, with other fighter markings created by squadron or group. XIII BC exercised some authority over its group markings: a May 1945 memo mentioned that tail markings were being changed by a XIII BC letter, but the scope of the letter itself remains unclear. There was certainly never a common system for the Thirteenth's bomb group markings.

In June 1944 the Far East Air Forces (plural)(FEAF) was created to coordinate operations between the Fifth and Thirteenth Air Forces. A command structure was formalized, and some logistical and training functions were changed. In most respects the larger Fifth AF became the primary assault force, while the Thirteenth became the support force. (By January 1945, there were suggestions that the Thirteenth should be disbanded and its units absorbed by the Fifth, but the logistical difficulties of such a reorganization precluded the event.) Some Seventh AF units were also assigned to FEAF in July 1945 in preparation for the

A P-38 of the 36th FS, 8th FG. Angled wing bands are black, while tail tips are white with black borders. Philippines, 1945. (Foote)

invasion of Japan. Although headquarters aircraft often carried the FEAF insignia, FEAF apparently exercised little influence over the markings of its subordinate commands.

In 1944 the Twentieth AF, commanded from Washington, began strategic B-29 missions against Japan. Planners scheduled the Twentieth to control five fighter groups in the Marianas under the 301st FW. Unit assignments were completely revised, but the planned plane-in-wing numbers remained with four of the original groups through VJ-Day: 51-199 for the 15th FG, 200-349 for the 21st FG, 350-499 reserved for the 318th FG, 500-649 for the 506th FG, and 650-799 for the 414th FG.

In the following listings, each unit is noted with its parent air force(s), group and squadron nicknames, assigned squadrons, squadron colors, and aircraft number ranges. Charts of standardized fighter markings appear on pages 68 & 69; bomber markings are on pages 72 & 73. (Twentieth B-29s are covered on page 83.)

FIGHTER MARKINGS OF THE PACIFIC BASIN

8th FG (V AF): P-39s wore squadron-color spinners and fin tips, and aircraft numbers/letters in Australia and New Guinea from March 42. All squadrons had P-38s by early 44. Squadrons were designated by angle and color of wing bands and squadron-color spinners by mid-1944. **35th FS** (Yellow): P-40s assigned in June 43. **36th FS** (White, later black): The only 8th FG P-39s with white tails. A white nose ring carried over to cowl flaps of the P-47s assigned in October 43. Early OD P-38s used a white nose ring and two horizontal white tail bands. **80th FS** (Gray, Green)(Headhunters): P-39s with shark mouths, replaced by P-38Fs in February 43.

15th FG (VII AF): In Hawaii with two fuselage bands, February 42; two nose bands by mid-43. Squadron assignments and locations varied. P-47s assigned in early 44, with squadron-designed markings by July; P-51s in November 44, to Iwo Jima in February 45. **6th NFS**: Assigned March 43-June 44. **12th FS** (1-25): P-39s on Christmas Island were assigned to the 15th in August 42. To SOPAC November 42, reassigned to 18th FG in March 43. **45th FS** (Light green; 50-99)(Trail Blazers): Sand and blue P-40Ns on Canton Island, September 43. Back to Hawaii in April 44. **46th FS** (White; 100-149): Sand and

The 8th FG's 35th FS briefly transitioned to P-40s in June 1944. The yellow squadron color was carried on spinners, but not repeated on fin tops. Cape Gloucester, New Britain. (USAF)

blue P-39s on Canton, March 43. To Makin December 43, repainted OD/Gray. Back to Hawaii February 44, transferred to 21st FG June 44. **47th FS** (Lt blue, later black; 150-199)(Dogpatchers): P-36 and P-40 in Hawaii. **78th FS** (Yellow; 200-249, P-51s 100-149)(Bushmasters): Midway P-40Ks assigned in March 43, returned to Hawaii in April.

18th FG (VII AF; XIII AF)(Ringmaster Fighter Group): Seven squadrons in Hawaii by October 42, when 3 moved to the 318th FG. Single band aft of wing. Released all squadrons March 43 and moved to SOPAC. All P-38s by June 44. Aircraft numbers to tails in January 45, with squadron-color radiator checks May 45. **6th FS**: Hawaiian P-40s, to P-70s (6th NFS) January 43; to 15th FG March 43. **12th FS** (200-249 on P-38s): SOPAC P-39s and some P-38s to 18th command in March 43. **19th FS** (The Diamondhead Squadron): Hawaiian P-40s with diamond on aft fuselage. To 318th FG in March 43. **44th FS** (Yellow, 400-425 on late P-38s)(Vampires): Hawaiian P-40s with horizontal bar aft of star. To 318th FG October 42, then to SOPAC. 18th command again in March 43. Mix of P-40s, P-38s, and P-39s until November 43, then all P-38s. **70th FS** (300-350; 100-150 on NMF P-38s)(White Knights): On Fiji, but assigned P-39/P-38 in combat with 347th FG from Guadalcanal; to 18th March 43. Moved to Guadalcanal in April 43. P-39s and P-40s until June 44, then NMF P-38s. **72nd FS**: Hawaiian P-40s to 318th FG in October 42. **73rd FS**: P-40s to Midway, June 42. To 318th FG October 42. **78th FS**: Hawaiian P-40s replaced the 73rd FS on Midway, January 43. To 15th FG, March 43. **333rd FS**: Activated August 42. P-39s to Canton Island September 42. To 318th FG January 43.

21st FG (VII AF): Activated in Hawaii with 3 P-39 squadrons in June 44; single nose stripe and numbers 500-649. P-38s with squadron color spinners saw combat on Saipan with the 318th FG. P-51Ds in January 45 to Iwo Jima in April. **46th FS** (P-51s Blue, 200-249): Assigned from 15th FG. **72nd FS** (Yellow, 250-299)(The Scalpers): Assigned from 318th FG. **531st FS** (Red on P-39s, white on P-51s; 300-349): Assigned from VII FC.

35th FG (V AF): After decimation in the Philippines, the 35th FG reorganized in February 42 with new P-39s with squadron-color spinners and tail tips. Transition to P-47s in November 43, with aircraft numbers on the fuselages and squadron-color nose flashes. With fuselage stripes, numbers moved to the tail (eventually inside horizontal

(Above) Reinforcing Canton Island, a P-40K of the 45th FS, 15th FG launches from the escort carrier USS Breton. The aircraft, a recent transfer, still bears the nose markings of the 78th FS. (Lambert)

(Above)15th FG P-47s briefly used two thin nose rings (one at the cowl lip and one around the cowl flaps) in early 1944. Fuselage number 204 and yellow nose bands indicate the 78th FS. (USAF)

(Below) By mid-44, the 15th's squadrons had devised more elaborate markings. For the 78th, wing tips, cowl, and tail tips were black and yellow. The Bushmaster emblem appeared on both sides of the cowl. (Lambert)

band). Similar P-51 markings March 45. **39th FS** (Light blue; 10-39): Switched to P-38Fs in October 42 with nose and tail numbers and nacelle shark mouths. **40th FS** (Red; 40-69): Red lightning bolt on P-47 tails. **41st FS** (Buff on P-39, yellow on P-47/P-51, green postwar; 70-99).

49th FG (V AF): Three-digit P-40 tail numbers in Australia, two-digit numbers by June 42. Squadron-color spinners and some painted fins and fin tips. Switched to P-38s in late 44. **7th FS** (Blue; 11-39): One P-40 flight marked "Nick Nichols' Nip Nippers" over exhausts and often wore shark mouths. Several NMF P-40s during P-38 conversion

Squirt was the personal P-51 of James Beckwith, 15th FG commander. The 15th's COs traditionally carried aircraft number 15; remaining markings belonged to the 47th FS. (Lambert)

on Biak September 44. **8th FS** (Yellow, black on NMF; 40-69): P-38s September 44. **9th FS** (White, red on NMF; 70-99): P-38Fs January 43 with nose/fin numbers. P-47s with white ring at cowl lip in November 43. New P-38s in April 44.

51st FG (FEAF): After CBI combat, the 51st reactivated on Okinawa in October 46. P-47Ns wore colors of earlier units (primarily the 507th FG). Squadron color cowl rings. **16th FS** (Blue); **25th FS** (Red); **26th FS** (Yellow)

54th FG (XI AF): Air echelon took P-39s to Alaska, June-December 42. The **42nd FS** and **56th FS** carried nose numbers from 10-66. **57th FS** used a wolf head emblem.

58th FG (V AF): P-47s to the SWPA in November 43 with squadron color cowls and white fuselage codes. Horizontal band cowl markings mid-44. Fuselage codes were over painted by stripes and not reapplied. **69th FS** (White, later red; A1-A33). **310th FS** (Yellow; H34-H66): cowl completely yellow. **311th FS** (Blue; V67-V99). **201st Mexican Fighter Sq** (White): Attached, often used Mexican national markings.

318th FG (VII AF): Activated in October 42 with three former 18th FG squadrons, wearing a single nose band. P-47Ds with squadron-color band aft of cockpit in April 44; cowl lip, wing tip, and tail bands added later. To Saipan June-July 44. Squadron-colored outer thirds of tails with NMF P-47Ns April 45. Black/yellow group tail stripes with squadron-color cowl rings June 45. **19th FS** (Robin Egg Blue, Blue on P-47s; 301-349, A-Z on P-47Ds, 1-37 on P-47Ns): P-40s from 18th FG in March 43 (squadron traded for 44th FS). P-47Ds with paint stripped from cowls and vertical tails, and blue cowl flaps. Blue cowl flaps on P-47Ns. **44th FS**: P-40s in SOPAC on 318th's activation. Traded to 18th FG March 43. **72nd FS** (Yellow; 350-399): P-39s in Hawaii and Gilberts December 43-April 44. To 21st FG June 44. **73rd FS** (White, Black on NMF; 400-449, 1-37 on Saipan)(Bar Flies): P-40s in Hawaii. **333rd FS**: (Light Green, Yellow on P-47s; 450-499, P-47s unnumbered): P-39s on Canton from 18th FG January 43; to Hawaii April 43.

343rd FG (XI AF): P-40s of 11th FS and 18th FS moved from the 28th Composite Group to the XI FC in June 42; P-38s of 54th FS were

(Above) By mid-1945 the 18th FG marked its tails with aircraft numbers and its boom radiators with squadron-colored checkerboards. The 12th FS also used their squadron color (blue) for booms bands. (Bowers)

(Above) *Little Red Head*, a P-38L (44-24008) of the 531st FS, carried red spinners as the only squadron marking. Lightnings of the 21st FG deployed to Saipan with the 318th FG in late 1944. (USAF)

(Above) P-47s of the 35th FG originally carried squadron-colored nose flashes, with plane-in-group numbers on the rear fuselage and nose. Aircraft number 35 was photographed on Noemfoor, Dutch East Indies in July 1944. Note the early reapplication of rudder stripes. (Taylor)

(Below)The 21st FG's Mustangs carried tail bands, spinners, and wing and tail tips in squadron colors. The P-51s on the left are from the 46th FS (squadron color medium blue). (USAF)

(Above) With the addition of Philippine invasion stripes in October 1944, the 35th moved its aircraft numbers to the fin (later adding a horizontal band above and below the number). Very few uncamouflaged aircraft carried the theater's white tail markings. (Bowers)

(Above) The 35th's P-51s carried similar markings, though *Mickey* does not yet have the group flash behind its spinner. (USAF)

(Above) The 49th FG's P-38s carried squadron-color spinners and plane-in-group numbers on the nose and radiators. Many of the group's P-40s and P-38s carried conspicuous individual tail markings, often covering earlier unit markings on second-hand airframes. (Simmons)

(Below) In 1946 the 51st FG was reactivated on Okinawa. Most of its P-47Ns carried 318th and 507th FG markings: *Honey Child*, coded "B5," retains markings and mission symbols of the 465th FS. (Wolak)

attached in May. The 343rd FG took control in September 42 and the 344th FS joined in October. NMF P-38s with squadron-colored spinners and fin tips by June 45. **11th FS** (Aleutian Tigers): White vertical band centered on rudder, horizontally crossed by June 43. Tiger head, yellow spinner and white fuselage band prior to October 43. P-38s in late 43. **18th FS**: Yellow spinner fronts, white rudder band with centered horizontal bar on P-40s. Some ex-54th FG P-39s in 43, P-38s beginning in 43. P-40s phased out in 45. **54th FS**: P-38s with yellow nose tips and numbers. **344th FS**: P-40s traded for the older aircraft of the 11th and 18th squadrons on arrival October 42; yellow spinner and wing leading edge. Some P-38s from 44.

347th FG (XIII AF)(The Sunbusters Fighter Group): Activated on New Caledonia in October 42. All P-38s by July 44 without group marking system. **67th FS** (Yellow on P-38s; 1-61 on P-39s, 150-200 on P-38s): Shark mouths on Guadalcanal. NMF P-38s in April 44 with yellow spinners and tail tips and blue stripes bordering the radio call. Green lightning on tails in January 45. **68th FS** (Red)(Lightning Lancers): To Tongatabu with P-40Es from May-October 42; to 347th FG on Tontouta in November, and Guadalcanal in December. April-December 43 on Fiji as training squadron. P-39s to combat in January 44. P-38Js in June 44 with red spinners and red pencil stripes on the wing leading edges by August. **70th FS**: To Fiji with P-39s; pilots flew P-39s and P-40s over Guadalcanal from September 43. To 18th FG in March 43. **339th FS** (100-150, later 10-50)(Sunsetters): P-38 squadron activated October 42 in SOPAC.

348th FG (V AF): First P-47s to the SWPA in June 43; squadron tail tip colors. Horizontal squadron-colored tail band in April 44. Fourth squadron added September 44; plane numbers reallocated. With addition of rudder stripes, tail band became vertical bar forward of rudder post. P-51Ds, from January 45, used same markings with squadron-color spinners. **340th FS** (Red; 1-25, later 10-39). **341st FS** (Yellow; 26-50, later 40-69). **342nd FS** (Blue; 51-75, later 70-99). **460th FS** (Black; 101-129).

413th FG (VII AF): P-47Ns with squadron/aircraft letters to Ie Shima in May 45. Playing card symbols initially on the rudders, later on fin with painted tails and cowls. **1st FS** (AA-AZ): Black rudder with silver diamond, black cowl ring and wing tips. Tails subsequently blue. **21st FS** (BA-BZ). **34th FS** (CA-CZ): White or yellow rudder with black spade. Later, yellow tails and cowl fronts.

414th FG (XX AF) P-47Ns to Iwo Jima in June 45. Black eighteen-inch rear fuselage band with the tail and cowl in squadron-colors. **413th FS** (650-699). **437th FS** (700-749). **456th FS** (750-799).

475th FG (V AF): P-38s to New Guinea in August 43. Tail tips and spinners in squadron-colors. **431st FS** (Red, 110-139)(Satan's Angels): **432nd FS** (Yellow, 140-169). **433rd FS** (White, light blue on NMF, 170-199)(Blue Devils).

506th FG (XX AF): P-51Ds to Iwo Jima in April 45. Aft fuselages (exclusive of control surfaces) diagonally striped in squadron colors. Switch to solid colors began in May 45. **457th FS** (500-549): (The original red squadron color was changed to green before tail stripes were applied.) **458th FS** (550-599). **462nd FS** (600-649).

   507th FG (VII AF)(The Rainbow Group): P-47Ns to Ie Shima 46 days before the War's end. Yellow tails and wing bands with blue squadron symbols. **463rd FS** (100-131). **464th FS** (132-169). **465th FS** (170-199).

   508th FG (VII AF): To Hawaiian defense force in January 45. Ex-15th/318th FG P-47Ds with fuselage numbers. Several P-47Ns acquired May 45. P-51s for some 468th FS patrols after March 45. **466th FS**. **467th FS**. **468th FS**.

(Above) The 54th FG saw combat in Alaska between June and December of 1942. The 42nd and 56th fighter squadrons carried large yellow nose numbers, as seen on this P-39F. (Army)

(Left) 58th FG P-47s generally carried white on the vertical portions of the tail only. The 310th FS used an orange-yellow cowl (often with alternating cowl flaps, as seen here) with H-prefixed codes. (Simmons)

(Left) In the 318th FG, 19th FS P-47Ds were marked with blue tail bands and cowl flaps, and with paint stripped from the vertical tails and cowls. *Miss Mary Lou* was photographed on Saipan in 1944. The extra yellow stripe at the tip of each prop blade was used to identify certain models of Curtiss and Aeroproducts cuffed propellers. (USAF)

(Below) The other side of *Miss Mary Lou* on a different date. Four small yellow pineapples painted beneath the cockpit are mission markings. The wing blocks the black radio call number (325429) and white fuselage letter ("C"); aircraft number "29" is in black on the bottom front of the cowl. (USAF)

(Above) The 318th's 78th FS moved its P-47Ds to the Marianas via the carrier USS *Manila Bay* in June 1944. *Dee-Icer* carried white wing tips, cowl edge, tail bands, and fuselage stripe, with the "Bar Flies" squadron emblem on the nose. (USAF)

(Right) P-47Ns of the 318th originally wore cowl fronts and tips of tail planes painted in squadron colors. Bitter, of the 19th FS, carries a modification of the pre-war emblem, with a "fiercer" fighting cock. (Swihart via Lloyd)

(Right) In June 1945, all 318th FG squadrons adopted black and yellow tail stripes with squadron-colored cowl fronts, though this 333rd FS P-47N has not yet received its yellow nose. (Rasmussen via Foote)

(Below) By 1945 the 343rd FG's four squadrons flew NMF P-38s. Though this pair of Lightnings served with the 54th FS, markings and colors have eluded accurate interpretation. (USAAF)

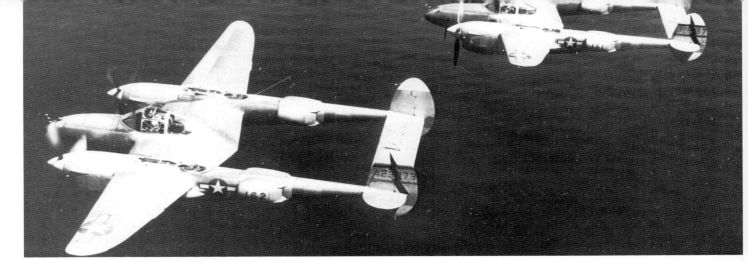

(Above) P-38 markings of the Thirteenth AF's 347th FG are also poorly documented. From January 1945 67th FS Lightnings carried yellow spinners and tail tips, with green lightning bolts on the fins. (USAAF)

(Left) The 348th FG made brief use of a squadron-colored horizontal band on the vertical tail. The red band belonged to the 340th FS. (Bowers)

(Left) With the addition of rudder stripes, the 348th switched to vertical tail bands. This P-51D carries the yellow band of the 341st FS. (Bowers)

(Below) A yellow tail, with a black spade, and a yellow forward cowl mark the 413th FG's 34th FS. A two-letter fuselage code, beginning with a "C", is blocked by the wing. (Terrien)

(Above) Central Pacific fighters often flew with partially-applied markings. This 414th FG P-47N has the black/yellow checks of the 437th FS painted on the forward cowl, with only the yellow added to the tail. The aircraft number has not yet been added to the fuselage. (Britt)

(Right) A second 414th FG P-47N displays 456th FS markings and insignia. Black lines on the wing leading edge helped pilots gauge dive angles: measuring from the wing tips, the lines gauge 20, 35, 50, and 70 degrees. (Britt)

(Right) Captain J. T. McKeon poses with his 475th FG P-38 Regina Coeli. White aircraft numbers, repeated on the tail, are from the 433rd FS's range (170-199); aft sections of the spinners are light blue with thin white edges. (Cavanagh)

(Below) *Wanda* was another 475th FG Lightning. Tail tips, the number "125", and the aft segment of the spinner are red. The 431st FS's "Satan's Angels" emblem is on the radiator and the nose tip. (Simmons)

(Above) A P-51D of the 462nd FS, 506th FG, is pushed across Iwo Jima's pierced steel planking. Note the masked area of the serial number, where traces of the earlier yellow tail stripes are still seen. (USAF)

(Left) The 458th FS kept its blue tail stripes longer than the 506th's other two squadrons. Photographed in July or August of 1945, number 550 is one of the few 458th Mustangs to wear the solid blue tail. (Britt)

(Left) Yellow wing bands and tails marked the 507th FG. Blue triangles identify these P-47Ns as members of the 463rd FS. (Terrien)

(Below) The 508th FG, the highest-numbered fighter group in the USAAF, joined the Hawaiian defense force in 1945. Other than large two-digit fuselage numbers, these P-47Ds show few alterations to the markings they carried with the 15th and 318th FGs.

The Bea, P-40E-1 of Lt F. J. Teahan, 8th FS, 49th FG, Port Moresby, New Guinea.

WAHL EYE II ("*PAT*"), P-400 of Lt Eugene Wahl, 39th FS, 35th FG, Twelve Mile Aerodrome, New Guinea.

port side

Old Maid, B-17E, 11th BG, Guadalcanal, wearing Hawaiian Air Depot Camouflage.

TOKYO JO, B-25D, 11th BS, China, February 1943.

Hyde's Harlot, P-40K of Capt Gordon Hyde, 78th FS, 15th FG, Hawaii.

33

NIGHT FIGHTER MARKINGS OF THE PACIFIC BASIN

After a fitful start with flat black P-70s, searchlight-guided P-38s, and even a few B-25s, the Pacific forces received their first P-61s in May 1944. Early P-61s were OD and Neutral Gray, the night fighter scheme approved in October 1943. Subsequent Jet Black P-61s often suffered from poor priming and substandard paints which led to excessive chipping, a problem compounded by the abrasive effects of coral sand.

6th NFS (VII AF)(Dark Blue, 16-49): P-70s in Hawaii beginning in September 42. Det B went to Guadalcanal in February 43 and Det A to New Guinea in April. P-61s over Saipan and Hawaii from June 44. White 2-digit nose numbers in Hawaii in April 45.

418th NFS (V AF, XIII AF from November-December 44): To New Guinea in November 43 with P-70s and P-38s taken from Det A, 6th NFS. Also used some B-25s during 1944. P-61s in September 44. To the Philippines in November 44. Tail markings were a diagonal, white-bordered, blue tail band with a yellow star and crescent moon. Squadron emblem carried by July 45.

419th NFS (XIII AF)(300-330)(Black Spiders): To the Solomons in November 43, with P-38s and P-70s taken from Det B, 6th NFS. P-61s

A P-61B of the 418th NFS shines in the Philippine sun. Tail markings are a white-bordered blue band with a yellow crescent moon (masked by the wing) and a yellow star. Only four digits of the radio call number are carried; the serial (42-39661) should have been presented as "239661." (Hensley via Taylor)

arrived in May 44. P-38s, P-70s, and hacks used white nose numbers 300-309. A detachment moved to New Guinea in June 44. Plane numbers moved to the tail starting in February 45. Squadron to the Philippines in March 45. White/red/white diagonal boom bands in April 45.

421st FS (V AF): P-70s and P-38s moved to New Guinea in January 44. P-61s arrived in June 44. Squadron to the Philippines in October. To Ie Shima in July 45. At least one aircraft carried yellow spinners and cowl flaps.

547th NFS (V AF): P-61s to New Guinea September 44, to the Philippines in January 45, and to Ie Shima in August 45. Spinners and cowl flaps appear to have been in flight colors.

548th NFS (VII AF): P-61s to Hawaii in September 44. Detachments to Saipan and Iwo Jima in February 45. To Ie Shima in June. Squadron emblem on nose, with red spinners and cowl flaps.

549th NFS (VII AF): P-61s to Hawaii in October 44. Detachments to Saipan and Iwo Jima in March 45. Emblem on nose with painted cowl flaps and spinners.

550th NFS (XIII AF)(330-359): P-61s to New Guinea in December 44. Emblem on tail, with white plane number on nose. Some use of P-38s and P-70s. Later markings of horizontal, white-bordered, red tail band. Wing tips, cowl flaps, and spinners in flight colors.

The 548th NFS's Black Widows carried red spinners and cowl flaps, with a "stalking cat" emblem on the nose. Iwo Jima, March 1945. (USAF)

A P-61 of the 419th NFS warms up in the Philippines, February, 1945. The 419th's aircraft carried a white number (300 to 329) on the nose or tail. Within two months the squadron began carrying diagonal red and white bands on the booms. (USAAF)

BOMBER MARKINGS OF THE PACIFIC BASIN

3rd BG (V AF)(Grim Reapers): To Australia in early 42 with various aircraft; all A-20s by January 44. Squadron-color tail tops, white plane letters on fins. Same markings on A-26s in July 45. **8th BS**: A-24s in February 42, A-20s by mid-42, and B-25s with white tail letters by March 43. **13th BS**: B-25s in February 42, some with skull noses by June 43. **89th BS**: A-20s in mid-42, B-25s by March 43. **90th BS**: B-25s in February 42, shark mouth by March 43, also seen on some A-20s.

5th BG (VII AF; XIII AF)(Bomber Barons): B-17s and B-18s in Hawaii, to SOPAC in November 42. 31st BS and 394th BS to B-24s in August 43. Blue shield tail markings with squadron-color band in October 44. Geometric symbols in May 45. **23rd BS** (01-25). **31st BS** (26-50). **72nd BS** (51-75). **394th BS** (76-99). **Snoopers** SB-24 Snoopers with flat black bellies assigned to group HQ as "5th BG Project" in October 43. Became the 868th BS (see page 38) in January 44.

11th BG (VII AF): B-17s and B-18s in Hawaii, December 41. To SOPAC in July 42, back to Hawaii for B-24 transition in March 43. Tail markings by June 44. **26th BS, 42nd BS, 98th BS, 431st BS.**

19th BG (V AF): After the fall of the Philippines and Dutch East Indies, the 19th flew B-17s, B-24s, and LB-30s from Australia. Returned to US in October 42, later flying B-29s with XX AF. **28th BS, 30th BS, 93rd BS, 435th BS.**

22nd BG (V AF)(The Red Raiders): B-26s in Australia in April 42, some with squadron-colored fin tips. B-25s in January 43. 19th BS took NMF B-26s back to combat in June 43. Group flew B-24s after January 44. Squadron-color fin bands with aircraft letter. Emblem on left nose by December 44, background in squadron-color; letters replaced by last three or four of serial. **2nd BS**: Emblem in B-25 fin band. **19th BS** (Silver Fleet). **33rd BS. 408th BS.**

27th BG (V AF) Early A-24s and B-25s in Australia. Returned to US May 42.

28th BG (XI AF) The 28th Composite Group in Alaska became the 28th BG in December 43. **11th FS** and **18th FS**: See 343rd FG. **21st BS**: Attached January 42 to September 43 with B-24s. **36th BS**: B-17s and B-24s, moved to Europe in November 43; **73rd BS**: B-26s and B-25s, to Second AF (Continental US) in October 43. **77th BS**: B-26s and B-25s. **404th BS** (Pink Elephants): B-24s.

30th BG (VII AF)(Atoll Busters): B-24s to Hawaii October 43. Tail markings in June 43. Back to Hawaii in March 45. **21st BS**: detached to 28th BG in January 42, inactivated November 43. **27th BS, 38th BS, 392nd BS, 819th BS.**

38th BG (V AF): Two B-25 squadrons to SWPA in September 42 (with 69th and 70th BSs to 42nd BG). 822nd and 823rd BSs assigned

An A-20G (42-54116) of the 3rd BG (or 3rd Attack Group, as it was known in the Fifth AF). The tail tip is green, the color of the 89th BS. (Simmons)

April 43. Monster faces on 71st and 405th BS planes mid-43; other squadrons by September 44. Squadron-color segments of tails. **71st BS** (Wolf). **405th BS** (Dragon). **822nd BS** (Panther). **823rd BS** (Tiger).

41st BG (VII AF): B-25s to Hawaii in October 43. Tail markings by April 45. **47th BS, 48th BS, 396th BS, 820th BS.**

42nd BG (XIII AF)(Wilson's Horses in October 43; The Crusaders in April 45): B-26s of **69th BS** and **70th BS** (detached from the 38th BG) to SOPAC in June 42. B-25s and assignment to the 42nd (still based in US) came in February 43. Group HQ, **75th BS**, and **390th BS** came to SOPAC in March 43. **106th RS (Bomb)**, which joined XIII AF in November 43, was attached in January 44, renamed **100th BS** in May 44, and assigned in February 45. Tail markings by April 45. Tail tops in (unidentified) squadron colors.

43rd BG (V AF)(Ken's Men): B-17s to SWPA, August 42, many with black bellies for night missions. Transition to B-24s starting in May 43, including 63rd BS Snooper SB-24s. Tail markings applied in April 44. **63rd BS** (Seahawks); Flat black bellies, later overall Jet Black. **64th BS, 65th BS, 403rd BS.**

90th BG (VII AF; V AF)(Jolly Rogers): B-24s in Hawaii, September 42; to SWPA November 42. Fins black below serials with white skull and crossed bombs in September 43. Squadron-color fins by mid-44, with last three of serial in white above the skull. **319th BS. 320th BS** (Moby Dick Squadron): Sharkmouths. **321st BS. 400th BS.**

307th BG (VII AF; XIII AF)(The Long Rangers): B-24s to Hawaii in October 42. To SOPAC, February 43. "LR" tail markings and squadron-color tail tips by mid-44. **370th BS, 371st BS, 372nd BS, 424th BS.**

312th BG (V AF)(The Roarin' 20s): SWPA October 43; P-40 patrols before taking A-20s in February 44. White band at base of fin, white aircraft letter on rudder, and white squadron playing card symbol below tail; some use of skull and crossed bones at nose tip. **386th** and **387th** BSs equipped with B-32s June 45. **388th BS, 389th BS.**

319th BG (VII AF): From the MTO to the US in January 45. To Okinawa with A-26s in July 45. Some blue vertical tails with white two digit numbers. **437th BS** (1-25). **438th BS** (26-50). **439th BS** (51-75). **440th BS** (76-99).

345th BG (V AF)(Air Apaches): To SWPA with B-25s, June 43. White squadron bands and squadron-color cowl rings applied in August 43. Faces on some B-25s, September 43. 498th, 499th, and 501st BSs dropped white tail markings for tail emblem July 44. **498th BS** (Falcons), **499th BS** (Blue Bats), **500th BS** (Rough Raiders), **501st BS** (Black Panthers): No monster design, though some ex-38th BG panthers were used.

380th BG (V AF)(The Flying Circus): B-24s to Australia, May 43;

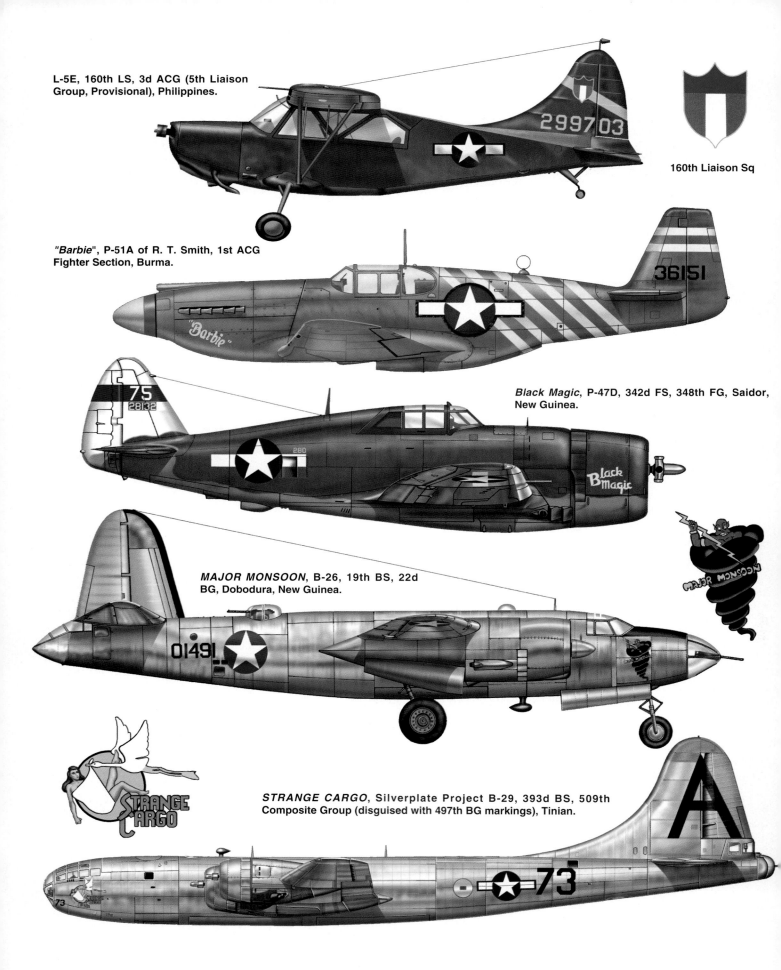

L-5E, 160th LS, 3d ACG (5th Liaison Group, Provisional), Philippines.

160th Liaison Sq

"Barbie", P-51A of R. T. Smith, 1st ACG Fighter Section, Burma.

Black Magic, P-47D, 342d FS, 348th FG, Saidor, New Guinea.

MAJOR MONSOON, B-26, 19th BS, 22d BG, Dobodura, New Guinea.

STRANGE CARGO, Silverplate Project B-29, 393d BS, 509th Composite Group (disguised with 497th BG markings), Tinian.

FIFTH AIR FORCE

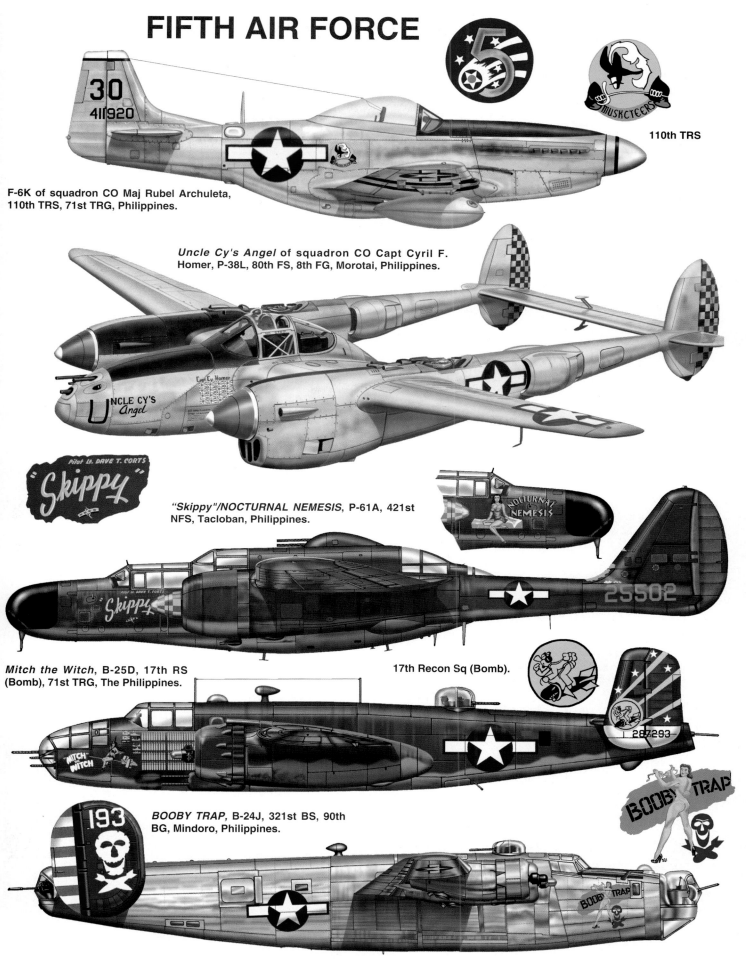

110th TRS

F-6K of squadron CO Maj Rubel Archuleta, 110th TRS, 71st TRG, Philippines.

Uncle Cy's Angel of squadron CO Capt Cyril F. Homer, P-38L, 80th FS, 8th FG, Morotai, Philippines.

"Skippy"/NOCTURNAL NEMESIS, P-61A, 421st NFS, Tacloban, Philippines.

Pilot Lt. DAVE T. CORTS
"Skippy"

Mitch the Witch, B-25D, 17th RS (Bomb), 71st TRG, The Philippines.

17th Recon Sq (Bomb).

BOOBY TRAP, B-24J, 321st BS, 90th BG, Mindoro, Philippines.

(Above and Below) *Miss Ileene*, a B-24M (44-42418), shows the 5th BG's post-May-1945 markings. The 23rd BS's square contains the radio call, with digits "4424" in red and "18" in white. Samar, Philippines. (AF Museum)

(Below) *Barrel House Bessie* was a B-24J (42-73027) assigned to the 431st BS, 11th BG. Tail stripes were yellow; cowl colors are uncertain, but the 11th BG was not known to use squadron colors. (Cleveland)

The 5th BG's early tail markings (from October 1944) displayed the blue shield of the "Bomber Barons". The diagonal stripe was in the squadron color, although the colors have not yet been identified. B-24J serial 44-40597. (AF Museum)

attached to RAAF until January 45. White-edged tail, quartered for each squadron in December 43; black without borders on silver aircraft. Circus squadron designs in February 44. Lion on fin with squadron-colored rudder or rudder band in June 45. **528th BS, 529th BS, 530th BS, 531st BS**.

407th BG (Dive)(XI AF): 632nd and **633rd Bomb Squadrons (Dive)** to Alaska with A-24s without unit markings in July 43. Both squadrons returned to Florida in August 43.

417th BG (V AF)(Sky Lancers): To the SWPA with A-20s in January 44. White rudder letters and squadron-color diagonal fin segments in March 44. **672nd BS, 673rd BS, 674th BS, 675th BS**.

494th BG (VII AF): B-24s to the Central Pacific in June 44. Tail markings applied by September 44. **373rd BS** in from CBI in July 45. **864th BS** (Kelly's Cobras), **865th BS, 866th BS, 867th BS**.

58th BS/531st FBS (VII AF): Hawaiian A-20s with "58B" designators at the beginning of the war. A-24s received in May 43. Redesignated 531st FBS in August 43. Received P-39s as the 531st FS in February 44. Transferred to the 21st FG in June 44.

868th BS (XIII AF): Flat black Snooper B-24s to HQ XIII AF from the 5th BG in January 44. Later Jet Black scheme with "Diamond-S" tail markings.

(Above) B-24Ds of the 28th BG warm up under gray Alaskan skies. The "Pink Elephants" nose emblem was carried by the group's 404th BS. (Simmons)

(Right) 27th and 38th BS B-24s parked on Kwajalein in June 1944. Several of these 30th BG planes have tail markings repeated over their right wings. (USAF)

(Right) Anguar in the Carolinas served as home for the B-24Js and Ls of the 22nd BG in December 1944. Squadron-colored tail bands appear on most aircraft, with the Red Raider emblem being applied on a squadron-colored shield on the left side of each nose. (USAF)

(Below) A trio of 38th BG B-25Gs heads for combat over New Guinea. All wear the yellow lower tails of the 822nd BS, though only the lead Mitchell sports Black Panther nose markings. (Cooper)

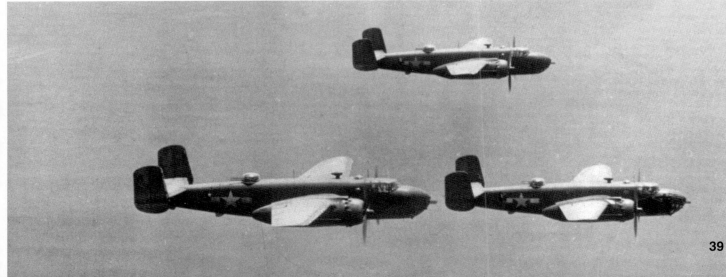

SEVENTH AIR FORCE

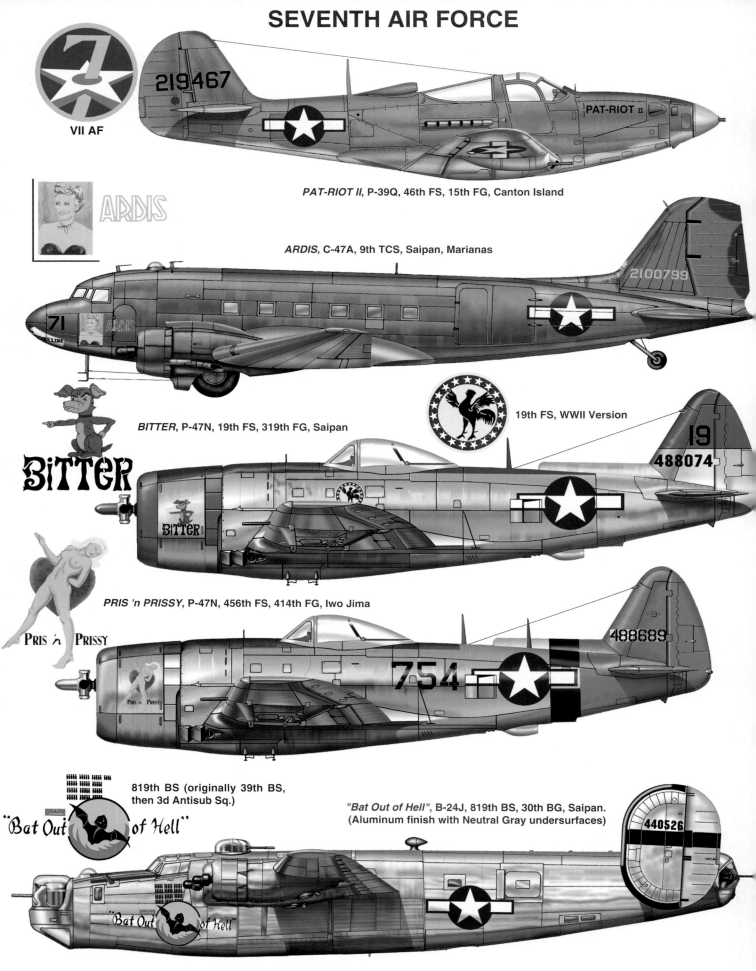

VII AF

PAT-RIOT II, P-39Q, 46th FS, 15th FG, Canton Island

ARDIS, C-47A, 9th TCS, Saipan, Marianas

BITTER, P-47N, 19th FS, 319th FG, Saipan

19th FS, WWII Version

PRIS 'n PRISSY, P-47N, 456th FS, 414th FG, Iwo Jima

819th BS (originally 39th BS, then 3d Antisub Sq.)

"Bat Out of Hell", B-24J, 819th BS, 30th BG, Saipan. (Aluminum finish with Neutral Gray undersurfaces)

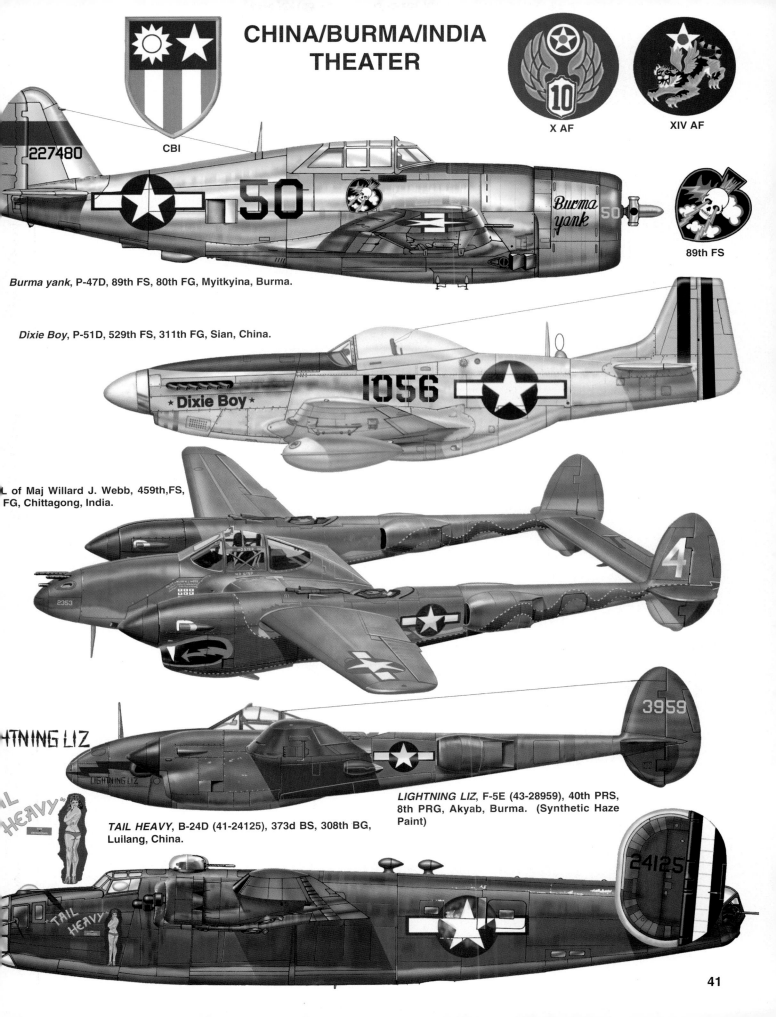

CBI

X AF

XIV AF

89th FS

227480

Burma yank

50

Burma yank, P-47D, 89th FS, 80th FG, Myitkyina, Burma.

Dixie Boy, P-51D, 529th FS, 311th FG, Sian, China.

★ Dixie Boy ★

1056

L of Maj Willard J. Webb, 459th,FS,
FG, Chittagong, India.

2353

4

3959

HTNING LIZ

LIGHTNING LIZ

LIGHTNING LIZ, F-5E (43-28959), 40th PRS,
8th PRG, Akyab, Burma. (Synthetic Haze
Paint)

IL
HEAVY

TAIL HEAVY, B-24D (41-24125), 373d BS, 308th BG,
Luilang, China.

TAIL HEAVY

24125

A B-25J of the 48th BS, 41st BG on Iwo Jima, June 1945. (USAF)

(Left) When the 41st BG adopted tail markings in April 1945, the 47th BS distinguished itself by *not* carrying any unit tail markings. (USAF)

(Left) A B-25J (43-28012) of the Crusaders (42nd BG) runs up its engines as a storm approaches. Tail tip is in an unidentified squadron color. April 1945. (DIA)

B-24s of the 43rd BG wait at Ie Shima during the final weeks of the war. Tail markings of the 64th and 65th Bomb Squadrons are visible. (USAF)

Out Of The Night II was a B-24M of the 43rd BG's 63rd BS. The Seahawks used these modified Liberators for night anti-shipping missions. Color is overall Jet Black. Clark Field, Philippines, May 1945. (USAF)

(Right) B-24D *The Powers Girl* (42-72807) of the 90th BG. The Jolly Rogers used these black and white tail markings until mid-44, when fins were painted in squadron colors. The nose of this aircraft has been depot-modified with a second tail turret. (Moran)

(Right) A second 90th BG B-24D (42-63984) on Morotai in late 1944. The red fin color and shark mouth were representative of the 320th BS. (AFM)

This Olive Drab B-24J (44-40942) of the 307th BG carries Jet Black under surfaces for night missions. A radome is mounted forward of the bomb bay. (Sporn)

2d FS (Cmndo)	2d TTS	3d (P)(CACW)	4th PCS	6th NFS	7th FS
8th PRS	9th PRS	9th TTS	10th BS	10th AJRS	13th CCS
13th FS	14th CCS	14th TTS	16th FS	19th BS	19th TCS
21st BS	21st PRS	22d BS	24th CMS	26th FS	28th PRS
39th TCS	45th FS	47th FS	54th FS	54th TCS	55th WRS
57th FS	63d BS	64th TCS	65th BS	67th FS	71st FS
72d FS	73d FS	75th FS	80th FS	87th BS	90th FS (Early)
90th FS (Later)	98th BS	158th LS	316th BS	317th BS	320th TCS
322d TCS	333d FS	333d TCS	338th BS	341st FS	348th NFS

353d FS   357th FS   374th FS   398thFS   400th FS   418thFS

431st FS   432d FS   456th FS   458th BS   462d FS   463d FS

464th FS   465th FS   490th BS   491st BS   500th BS   501st BS

506th BS   528th BS   529th BS   530th BS   530th FS   531st BS

531st FS   548th NFS   549th NFS   550th NFS   618th BS   676th BS

677th BS   678th BS   864th BS   865th BS   874th BS   6th PRG

22d BG   23d FG (Early)   23d FG (Late)   40th BG   80th FG   312th BG

345th BG (Early)   345th BG (Late)   444th BG   462d BG   468th BG   AACS

Alaskan Dept   FEAF

AJRS: Air Jungle Rescue Squadron
BG/GS: Bombardment Group/Squadron
CACW: Chinese-American Composite Wing
CCS: Combat Cargo Squadron
CMS: Combat Mapping Squadron
FG/FS: Fighter Group/Squadron
CMNDO: Commando
LS: Liaison Squadron

NFS: Night Fighter Squadron
(P): Provisional
PCS/PRG: Photo Charting Squadron/Group
PRS: Photo Reconnaissance Squadron
TCS: Troop Carrier Squadron
TTS: Target Tug Squadton
WRS: Weather Reconnaissance Squadron

Mis-A-Sip, an A-20G (43-21429) of the 312th BG rests on Floridablanca at the end of hostilities. The upper tail markings indicate prior service with the 417th BG. (USAF)

(Left) The first 319th BG A-26 markings on Okinawa were 500-series tail numbers. By the War's end, several aircraft had begun carrying cobalt blue tails and two-digit aircraft numbers. Few aircraft carried any nose art or mission symbols. (Herder via Oyster)

(Left) The 500th BS began applying the squadron's snorting mustang emblem to the tails of its aircraft in May 1944. By July the group's Air Apache insignia had replaced the squadron emblem. (USAF)

345th BG B-25s carried "Air Apache" tail markings from July 1944. The Green Falcon painted on the nose identified the 498th BS. (Eppstein via Lloyd)

Beautiful Betsy displays the 380th BG's early tail markings. Many of the group's B-24s did not have white outlines on their tails. (Osborne)

(Right) *Kay* was an A-20G of the 417th BG. The diagonal fin segment was in the squadron color — in this case either the 672nd BS's red or the 675th BS's blue.

(Right and Below) A 494th BG B-24J leaves Mindanao after a March 1945 raid. *Shack Bunny* has the quartered tail of the 867th BS. The last three digits of the serial were reapplied in larger characters starting in February. (USAF)

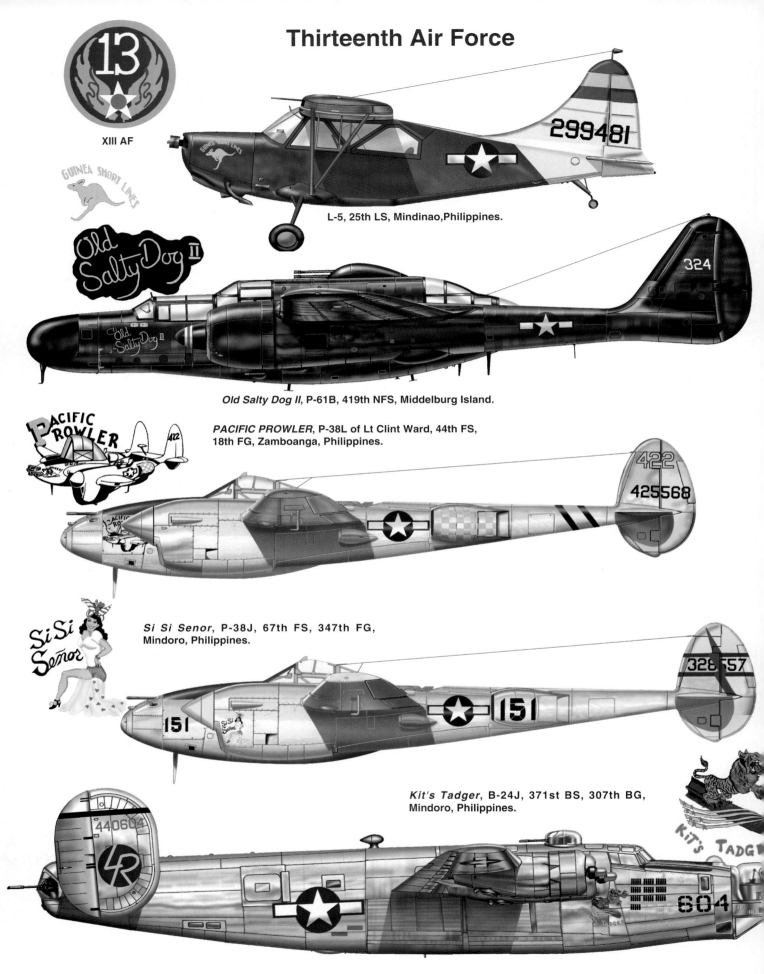

Thirteenth Air Force

XIII AF

L-5, 25th LS, Mindinao, Philippines.

Old Salty Dog II, P-61B, 419th NFS, Middelburg Island.

PACIFIC PROWLER, P-38L of Lt Clint Ward, 44th FS, 18th FG, Zamboanga, Philippines.

Si Si Senor, P-38J, 67th FS, 347th FG, Mindoro, Philippines.

Kit's Tadger, B-24J, 371st BS, 307th BG, Mindoro, Philippines.

TRANSPORT MARKINGS OF THE PACIFIC BASIN

During January 1943 *Duchess* arrived in New Guinea with the 317th TCG's 39th TCS (note the covered wagon emblem). All of the group's C-47s were subsequently transferred to the 374th TCG, which applied the white aircraft numbers aft of the cockpit. (USAF)

In January 1942 the Allied command in Australia organized its air transport activities under what became the Directorate of Air Transport (DAT). That April the Americans activated the 21st and 22nd Transport (later Troop Carrier) Squadrons under DAT's Air Courier Service. The "fleet" comprised war-weary bombers, former airliners, C-56 Lodestars, C-53s, and one C-39. New C-47s arrived in October with the 6th TCS, and the 374th TCG was activated in November to command the three squadrons. In December they were joined by the 33rd TCS (with more C-47s), fresh from six weeks on Guadalcanal. Under DAT, all 374th TCG aircraft tails displayed five-letter Australian civil codes as radio call signs in lieu of the (serial-derived) USAAF radio call numbers.

At year's end most of the group moved to New Guinea for the assault on Buna. When the 317th TCG arrived in January 1943, the new unit immediately traded its fresh C-47s for the 374th's older mounts. The 374th (which remained in New Guinea) began painting two-digit plane-in-group numbers aft of its cockpits, while the 317th joined DAT and flew with Australian registrations.

The Fifth AF activated the 54th TCW in March to control its tactical air supply units; the 374th was assigned as the wing's first group in May, but the 317th remained with DAT for some time. As new groups arrived in the SWPA, the 54th TCW assigned ranges of plane-in-wing numbers. (Most groups also painted rudder trim tabs in squadron colors.) The 375th TCG, arriving in July 1943, took numbers 100 to 199. The 403rd TCG joined the Thirteenth AF in August, but immediately transferred its 65th and 66th TCSs to the 54th TCW. Their C-47s took numbers 200 to 249. August also brought the 433rd TCG's C-47s, numbered 300 to 399 (skipping 251 to 299). The 433rd's headquarters caught up in October and took control of the 65th and 66th squadrons.

September 1943's airborne assault on Nadzab brought twenty-four 317th TCG C-47s to 54th TCW control; the aircraft were temporarily assigned numbers in the low 400s. At the end of the month the 374th and the 317th TCGs again traded assignments. The 317th TCG took aircraft numbers 6 to 99, while the 374th TCG (back under DAT) took numbers 500 to 599. In December 1944, the 2nd Combat Cargo Group (with C-46s) joined the 54th taking numbers 600 to 720. The 54th also controlled several service squadrons, independent squadrons, and the 21st Service Group: any of these might account for the mid-45 photos showing C-47 aircraft numbers in the 900s.

When DAT disbanded in October 1944 - reorganizing as FEAF's 5298th TCW (Prov.) - the 54th TCW ordered an "X" prefix added to its aircraft numbers as a distinguishing marking. With little space on the pilot's side, the "X" was often painted below the window until the entire code could be reapplied. Not to be outdone, in November the 5298th ordered a "W" placed above the center digit of the plane numbers on its US aircraft.

Squadron-by-squadron transition to C-46s began in October. For clarity on manifests, in December the 54th ordered that its C-46s would carry an "XA" prefix to the plane-in-wing number; C-47s would continue to use an "X" prefix. Similarly, 374th TCG C-46s used "WA" prefixes when C-46 transition began in April 1945. By March 1945 C-46s predominated the 54th and the codes were revised to "X" prefixes for C-46s and "X" prefixes with "A" suffixes for remaining C-47s.

On 30 December 1944 the 5298th TCW (Prov) was designated "322nd TCW" and assigned to Far East Air Service Command (FEASC). The 374th TCG remained the wing's only combat group. In May 1945 the 322nd dropped all 500-series numbers and began identifying aircraft by the last four digits of the serial (which were usually highlighted on the fin). A yellow "W" was centered on the fin above the radio-call number. Plane-in-group nose numbers were covered by a red FEASC arrow bearing the yellow characters "322 TCW".

317th TCG (V AF)(The Jungle Skippers): C-47s, C-46s from September 45. Four DDT spray C-47s carried no plane numbers. "Jungle Skippers" over cabin windows by June 45. **39th TCS, 40th TCS, 41st TCS, 46th TCS**.

374th TCG (V AF): Nose numbers assigned in order of squadron arrival. C-46s from April 45. Rudder trim tab colors: **6th TCS** (Red)(Bully Beef Express). **21st TCS** (White/Red/Yellow stripes). **22nd TCS** (Yellow). **33rd TCS** (White): Indian tribe nicknames.

375th TCG (V AF): **55th TCS, 56th TCS, 57th TCS** (TokyoTrolley), **58th TCS**.

Two of the three ex-KNILM (Royal Netherlands East Indies Airways) Lockheed 14s used by the 374th TCG at Ward's Drome, New Guinea, in December 1942. VH-CAJ was later redesignated as a C-111 (serial 44-83234) when the AAF completed its paperwork in 1943. (USAF)

FIFTH AIR FORCE TROOP CARRIER NUMBERS

SQUADRON AIRCRAFT NUMBER RANGES

								GROUP	DATES
6-25 21st TCS		**26-50** 22d TCS		**51-75** 6th TCS		**76-99** 33d TCS		374th TCG	Jan 43 - Sep 43
6-25 39th TCS		**26-50** 40th TCS		**51-75** 41st TCS		**76-99** 46th TCS		317th TCG	Sep 43 -VJ-Day
101-125 55th TCS		**126-150** 56th TCS		**151-175** 57th TCS		**176-199** 58th TCS		375th TCG	Jul 43 - VJ-Day
201-225 65th TCS		**226-250** 66th TCS						(attached to) 433d TCG	Aug 43 -Feb 45
300-325 67th TCS		**326-350** 68th TCS		**351-375** 69th TCS		**376-399** 70th TCS		433d TCG	Aug 43 -VJ-Day
401-425 C FLIGHT								317th TCG	Sep 43
500-525 6th TCS		**526-550** 21st TCS		**551-575** 22d TCS		**576-599** 33d TCS		374th TCG	Sep 43 - May 45
600-630 5th CCS		**631-660** 6th CCS		**661-690** 7th CCS		**691-720** 8th CCS		2d CCG	Nov 44 -VJ-Day

(This chart has been assembled from data in unit histories and missing aircrew reports.)

(Below) A C-47A of the 69th TCS, 433rd TCG over the mountains of New Guinea. Trim tab colors were used by most Fifth AF squadrons, though only a few squadrons' colors have been identified. (Cooper)

(Below) *Quivering Sal* was a C-46 of the 57th TCS, 375th TCG. In March 1945 the "XA163" aircraft code was revised to "X163" by painting out the "A" with fresh OD paint. At the same time, 54th TCW C-47 codes were modified with "A" suffixes. (USAF)

(Above) In December 1943, each squadron of the 317th and 375th TCGs received a war-weary B-17 for cargo drops over heavily contested areas. This B-17E of the 57th TCS crashed on landing at Aitape, New Guinea, May 1944. (Army)

403rd TCG (XIII AF); To SOPAC in August 43, taking control of the **13th TCS** (in theater) but loosing 65th and 66th TCSs to the SWPA. **63rd** and **64th TCS**s with black two-digit numbers (often outlined in white) on nose and engine nacelles. 13th TCS bore only a gold star on the nose tip or fin. Few group planes carried unit markings by late-44, when tail markings were revised to yellow stripes bordering the radio call, with white plane numbers in black squares on nose tips and fins. **65th** and **66th TCS**s returned February 45.

433rd TCG (V AF)(Frontline Airline): **65th TCS** and **66th TCS** (Flying Box Cars) to 403rd TCG in February 45. **67th TCS**, **68th TCS**, **69th TCS**, **70th TCS**.

2nd CCG (V AF): C-46s to the Philippines in November 44. **5th CCS**, **6th CCS**, **7th CCS**, **8th CCS** attached to 322nd TCW, November 44-January 45.

9th TCS (VII AF)(The Victory Line): C-47s to Hawaii in February 44. Noses with black or white numbers 41-75 and white "baggage label" with "The Victory Line" stenciled in black

19th TCS (VII AF)(Southern Cross Airways): Activated in Hawaii January 41 with C-47s and LB-30s.

42nd TCS (XI AF): C-47s to Alaska from May 42 to February 44.

54th TCS (XI AF)(Eager Beavers): C-47s to Alaska in November 42. Most aircraft with emblem on both sides of the nose.

311th TCS: 20 C-47Bs to Hawaii in February 1945. To Eighth AF Service Command on Okinawa in August 1945. To 54th TCW in February 1946, inactivating in May.

316th TCS: C-47s to Hawaii in November 1944. C-46s in 1945. To Eighth AF on Okinawa in September 1945; 54th TCW February 1946, Inactivated in March.

318th TCS (C): See 3rd Air Commando Group.

In May 1945 the 322nd TCW dropped aircraft numbers, replacing them with a red arrowhead and yellow "322 TCW". The white cowl markings (and rudder trim tab) with an Indian tribe nickname were exclusive to the 33rd TCS. (USAF)

This trio of 9th TCS C-46s was photographed on Kwajalein in July 1944. The 9th, known as "The Victory Line," was assigned directly to HQ Seventh Air Force. The 9th's white tag and "The Victory Line" nose marking were similar to the "TAG" (Transport Air Group) markings worn by Marine Corps R5Cs. (USAF)

(Below) A derelict 374th TCG C-47A rests beside the runway at Quezon, Manila, in early 1945. The "W" centered over the aircraft number signified the 322nd TCW, which directed the 374th as its only troop carrier group. The number 506 and the red trim tab identified the 6th TCS. (USAF)

(Above) A C-47A of the 374th's 33rd TCS rests at the end of the Henderson Field runway in March 1945. The white squadron trim tab was standard, but the "P" prefix has not been explained by unit records. (Archives via Lucabaugh)

Another C-46 of the 374th TCG, 322nd TCW, with the last four digits of the radio call number and highlighted as an aircraft number, and with the wing's "W" above. With the first two digits in red, the full radio call of this C-46D reads "478347". The 21st TCS trim tab colors are (from the top) white, red, and yellow. (Copp)

(Left) A DUKW is used to unload a 6th CCG C-46D (42-96780) after a takeoff accident at Morotai. The "W" beneath the serial (rather than an "XA" nose number) was used while the 8th CCS was briefly attached to the 322nd TCW. Trim tab markings appear to be yellow and black.

(Left) Paratroopers jump from Jungle Skippers (317th TCG) C-47s over Camalaniugan Air Strip, Luzon, on 23 June 1945. The "A" designator suffix had been added to all of the 54th TCW's remaining C-47s in March. (USAF)

As the 54th's C-47s added an "A" suffix, the wing's C-46s dropped their "XA" prefixes. On this C-46D of the 433rd TCG (the Frontline Airline), the entire aircraft number has been painted out and reapplied. Trim tab colors are yellow and light blue. (Britt)

Two 403rd TCG C-47As on Bougainville to evacuate wounded in December 1943. *Catfish,* on the right, carries the 13th TCS's gold star at the tip of its nose, a reminder of the squadron's Presidential Unit Citation. (USMC)

(Right) A C-47B of the 403rd drops supplies at Valencia, Mindanao, on 17 May 1945. Group tail markings by this date included two yellow bands bordering the serial and a plane-in-group number on a black square. (AAF)

(Right) A C-46 of the 7th CCS, 2nd CCG, performs a medevac mission in the Philippines. The squadron trim tab, not seen in this view, was solid green. (USAF)

(Below) 54th TCS C-47s operated over Alaska and the Aleutians from November 1942. Most aircraft, including this stripped C-47A, carried the squadron emblem on both sides of the nose. (USAF)

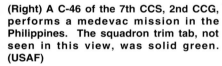

RECONNAISSANCE MARKINGS OF THE PACIFIC BASIN

4th PG (XIII AF): To SOPAC in November 42. Renamed 4th Photo Recon & Mapping Group in May 43, 4th PG (Recon) in November 43, and 4th RG in May 45. **4th PCS**: F-7s in the SWPA in November 44. Codes 4-A to 4-Z on noses. To 6th RG in May 45. **17th PRS**: F-5s to SOPAC in December 42. Renamed 17th PS (L) in February 43 and 17th PRS in November 43. [Unrelated to 17th RS (Bomb) of 71st TRG.] Tail emblem by 45. **18th PMS**: F-10s to SOPAC in January 43. Renamed 18th PS (H) in February 43 and 18th CMS in October 43. Inactivated February 44. **38th PRS** F-5s to SWPA in December 44.

6th PRG (V AF)(Hawkeyes): To SWPA in September 43, claiming the 8th RS. Named 6th Photo Recon & Mapping Group in May 43, 6th PRG in August 43, and 6th RG in May 45. Group emblem on tails of F-5s by 45. **8th PS**: Named 8th PRS in June 42, 8th PS (L) in February 43, and 8th PRS in November 43. F-4s to SWPA in April 42; "last two" on nacelles, red/white/blue spinners and trim tab stripes. Flew some B-17s and B-26s from 1942-44. NMF F-5s with fin tips striped red/white/blue, emblem on radiator, and "last three" on nacelle. **20th CMS** (Flying Dumbos): Renamed 20th RS (LR, Photo-RCM) in May 45. F-7s with yellow tail, with black winged camera replaced by a hawk in 45. **25th PRS**: F-5Bs in Haze Paint with last three on nose. Some

Bug-eyed *Singin' Sam* was an F-10 of the 18th CMS, which served with the Thirteenth Air Force from January 1943 to February 1944. The OD/Gray camouflage is unaltered by unit markings. (USAF)

B-25s in 44. **26th PRS**: F-5. **36th PRS**: F-5.

71st TRG (V AF): To the SWPA in November 43. Tactical recon squadrons flew P-39s and P-40s with squadron-color spinners and plane numbers on nose. TRSs converted to P-51/F-6, briefly with squadron-color wing bands. Squadron-color tail tips and spinners. **17th RS (Bomb)**: B-25s with white lower fins and bar at rudder hinge line. Post-June 44 markings on page 37. **25th LS** (Guinea Short Lines): L-5s with white kangaroo on left cowl. To XIII AF in February 45. Green/Yellow wing and tail in bands May 45. **82nd TRS** (Yellow; 40-75): P-51s in November 44. Late war black tail band and spinner. **110th TRS** (White, Black post-war; 10-39)(Musketeers): P-51s in February 45.

2nd PCS (FEAF): Renamed 2nd RS (LR, Photo) in June 45. Mapped Alaska with F-2s, F-3s and F-10s, the Caribbean with F-10s, and South America with A-29Bs. Double aircraft letters (AA, BB, etc.) with a variety of high visibility schemes. To FEAF with F-7s in October 44. Codes 2A to 2Z.

28th PRS (VII AF): F-5s to Hawaii in January 44. Nacelle emblems, flight letter and plane number on radiators. Black tails, plane letter in white diamond in June 45.

(Above) *Patched up Piece* was one of the 20th CMS's F-7s. The original Synthetic Haze camouflage has been stripped and the fuselage insignia has not yet been reapplied. The black squadron emblem on the yellow tail would later be replaced by the 6th RG's diving hawk. (USAF)

(Below) Three of the 6th RG's F-5 squadrons (25th, 26th, and 36th PRS) flew with the group's diving hawk as their only unit marking. (Taylor)

The three-point landing, as practiced by one 110th TRS P-40N pilot. The 110th used white prop spinners and aircraft numbers 10-39. Leyte, December 1944. (Army)

(Right) Early Mustang markings for the 71st TRG included spinners, tail tips, and diagonal wing bands in squadron markings. Yellow markings belonged to the 82nd TRS. (Bowers)

(Right) *Eyes of Texas* displays 28th PRS tail markings in June 1945. The black tail paint covers outboard stabilizers and two feet on either side of the inboard stabilizer. (USMC)

(Below) This 110th TRS F-6 shows its white squadron markings, with the group wing bands covered by black FEAF stripes. The Musketeer squadron emblem appears ahead of the fuselage insignia. (Lomer via AFM)

AIR COMMANDO MARKINGS OF THE PACIFIC BASIN

The Philly Pip, a red-nosed P-51D of the 4th FS (C). Tail is dark blue with a yellow "A". (McDaniel)

3d Air Commando Group (V AF): Moved to SWPA in October 44, by which time FEAF had little need for such a specialized unit. The liaison squadrons formed the **5th Air Liaison Group Commando (Prov)** from May-August 45. 318th TCS often flew under 54th TCW. P-51 vertical tails in dark or medium blue with yellow plane letters (in Greek or modern) and squadron-color spinners. **3d FS (C)** (Blue) **4th FS (C)** (Red). **318th TCS (C)** (A001-A025): Tail top white.

Nicknames in white cloud on nose. **157th LS (C):** To V AF in August 45. Red/white rudder stripes above L-5 serials, top red stripe over fin. Later markings (by July 45) of yellow tail top, with unidentified star insignia. **159th LS (C):** To V AF in August 45. L-5s with both "9" and thin vertical stripe on fin in flight colors (A - red, B - white, C - blue, and D - yellow). **160th LS (C):** L-5 tail emblem with diagonal yellow band.

Refueling on Luzon, *Charlotte 'M'* is a C-47 of the 318th TCS (C). The white tail tip and A-prefixed code were squadron markings, with most planes using a white cloud as backdrop for a nickname. May 1945. (USAF)

An L-5B of the 157th LS (C) over the Philippines in 1945. Fitting rudder stripes above the radio call number, most L-5s carried only eleven or twelve stripes. After the war this aircraft transferred to the 159th LS (C). (USAF)

More 157th LS L-5Bs, showing revised tail markings in June 1945. The fin insignia is unidentified, but does not resemble the squadron's jeep-driving grasshopper. (3rd ACG History)

MISCELLANEOUS UNIT MARKINGS OF THE PACIFIC BASIN

5th Emergency Rescue Group (V AF): Organized as 5276th Rescue Composite Group (Prov) in September 44 to coordinate rescue activities of the 3d ERS. Became the 5th ERG in March 45. **3d ERS**: OA-10s to Biak in September 44. **6th ERS**: OA-10s to the SWPA in June 44. Rescue B-17s often displayed "6th E.R.S." on radomes.

13th Emergency Rescue Group (XIII AF): Organized as 5230th Rescue Composite Group (Prov) in September 44 to coordinate rescue activities of the 2d ERS. Became the 13th ERG in March 45. **2d ERS**: OA-10s to the SWPA in July 44. Last two of serial on nose; blue/white stripes at tail tip. Rescue B-17s in 45.

14th Tow Target Squadron (XIII AF): To the SWPA with B-25s and some A-20s in January 45.

17th Tow Target Squadron (VII AF): B-26s, B-24s, C-78s, PQ-8s, and PQ-14s in Hawaii.

The 158th LS, the "Skyshark Fleet," didn't arrive in the Pacific until 1946. The squadron's L-5Es carried distinctive shark mouths. (158th LS History)

158th LS (Sky Shark Fleet)(V AF): L-5 courier service with occupation forces in Japan, October 46. Sharkmouth on most aircraft by late-47.

163d LS (VII AF): L-5s to Hawaii January 45; Okinawa May 45. No unit markings.

1st Glider Group (P): Nine CG-4 glider sections moved to the SWPA in November 44 to prepare for Philippine assaults. Organized as a *provisional* glider group (under the 54th TCW), the 1st was never constituted due to the cancellation of the planned airborne operations. The 2d and 6th Glider Sections disbanded in May 45. The 1st, 3d, 4th, 5th, 7th, 8th, and 9th Glider Sections disbanded in mid-45.

An L-5B of the Army ground forces takes off from an Okinawan strip in July 1945. Markings consist of two digits and an individual aircraft letter — a marking style also seen on Army liaison aircraft in Europe. (USAF)

One of the 2nd ERS's OA-10As on Mindanao in late 1945. The blue and white tail stripes were a squadron marking. A blue camouflage has been applied over the all-white factory scheme. (Leo M. Myers via Lucabaugh)

An aged B-24D, a PQ-14A, and a PQ-14B of the 17th Tow Target Squadron in formation over Oahu, April 1945. Despite the light tones in this black and white photo, the "Red Foxes" target aircraft are overall Insignia Red. (USAF)

CBI MARKINGS

In the China-Burma-India Theater the great battles against the Japanese were often overshadowed by the battles over control of AAF resources; conflicting and changing national priorities resulted in a command nightmare. The British were desperate to hold India and recover Hong Kong, Burma, and Singapore. The Soviets, not at war with Japan, supported the Chinese Communists and hoped to remove the existing Chinese government soon after defeating the Japanese. Chaing Kai-shek's Chinese government wanted to conserve supplies and troops for the war against the Communists while his Allies defeated Japan.

The original US goal envisioned Chinese troops, backed by American air power, driving the Japanese from China. But Chaing could not spare the manpower, and by 1943 Washington revised its goals: China could base B-29s for the strategic bombing of Japan; once defeated at home, the Japanese would relinquish captured Chinese territory. Chinese troops were asked to help retake Burma, opening ground and air routes for China's resupply.

US air units in the theater were controlled by the Tenth Air Force. American Claire Chennault, pre-war head of China's American Volunteer Group (AVG), was given command of the Tenth Air Force's China Air Task Force (CATF) in July 1942. Chennault believed that with enough planes, fuel, and supplies he could defeat the Japanese without a land campaign; Chaing, naturally, wanted Chennault to be assured of "enough." Chennault and his US military superiors had bitter differences over policy and tactics, a problem exacerbated by Chennault's willingness to bypass the chain of command and appeal directly to President Roosevelt through Chinese government connections. Finally, at the insistence of Chaing and over the objections of his military staff, Roosevelt established the Fourteenth Air Force on 10 March 1943, with Chennault as commander. To sidestep Chinese politics, the AAF gave two Washington-controlled organizations authority over two major operations: the Twentieth Air Force commanded all B-29s sent to the China, while ATC ran the "Hump" airlift resupply.

Markings in the CBI were often complicated by the transfer of aircraft between commands. From its earliest days, the Tenth overpainted the radio call numbers on the tails of its aircraft and substituted plane-in-group numbers. At some point in 1942, 23d FG (CATF) squadrons (including the attached 16th FS) began to use ranges of fifty numbers between 1 and 199. By the time the 51st FG moved to China in October 1943, the Fourteenth had initiated a system on plane-in-air-force numbers. Unit reassignments forced several changes, and no complete listing of the ranges has yet been found.

The P-51D of 23rd FG commander Ed Rector, in China during 1946. The three fuselage stripes (in squadron colors) recall the Air Corps' pre-war command markings. In the background are the "Pontiac" tail markings of the 76th FS. (Bowers)

In September 1944, Tenth AF fighters adopted the blue (or white on camouflage) wing, tail, and nose bands which would eventually become known as "Eastern Air Command stripes." (The Eastern Air Command coordinated the Tenth AF with the RAF Bengal Air Command.) The Fourteenth usually did not apply the markings, but sometimes inherited striped aircraft from the Tenth. Two other marking systems, both poorly documented, were carried by the Tenth Air Force at war's end. One involved a large letter "A" painted on fighter and bomber vertical tails (white on camouflage, and red or black on silver). The second system saw four yellow and three black stripes painted around the aft fuselages of B-24s and B-25s in India. The origins and purposes of these markings remain unknown.

The most famous of the theater's markings were the shark mouths introduced to the CBI by the AVG and its successor, the 23d FG. Several other CBI groups adopted toothed variations, although the 23d dropped its shark mouths late in 1944.

FIGHTER MARKINGS IN THE CBI

23d FG (X AF, XIV AF)(The Flying Tigers): Activated in July 42, growing out of the AVG. Aircraft marked with shark mouths, and with squadron-color fuselage stripes and spinners. Slowly converted to P-51s, starting November 43. Abandoned shark mouths in November 44, with new squadron P-51 designs. **16th FS**: Attached from the 51st FG from July 42 to October 43. **74th FS** (Red; 40-69, 10-50). **75th FS** (White; 151-200, 51-100)(Flying Sharks, Black-Tailed Bastards). **76th FS** (Blue; 10-39, 101-159)(Pontiac Squadron): Black/blue striped P-51 spinners. **118th TRS** (551-600, 151-200)(Black Lightning Squadron): To CBI January 44, attached to 23d FG from June 44 to August 45. Yellow-bordered black lightning bolts on P-51 fuselages. **449th FS** (301-350): Activated in CBI with P-38s in August 43; attached from 51st FG. Relieved October 43, but remained with 23d till May 44.

33d FG (X AF, XIV AF): From the MTO to India with P-47s in February 44. To China in April 44 (numbered 801-900) with squadron tail stripes. Returned to X AF in September 44 with EAC stripes. P-38 conversion beginning in November 44, retained 800 numbers. Plane-in-group numbers and large "A" on tails by August 45. **58th FS**: P-38s in January 44. **59th FS**: P-38s in March 45. **60th FS**: P-38 March 45. **459th FS** (50-99)(Twin Dragon Sq): P-38s transferred from 80th FG in May 45.

51st FG (X AF; XIV AF): The first AAF fighters in the CBI, March 42, with shark-mouthed P-40s. Assigned to XIV AF in October 43.

First P-51s assigned in March 44. Squadron tail marking designs. **16th FS** (10-39, 351-400)(Flying Wall of China Sq): Pre-War blue spinners, later white. **25th FS** (Red; 4-39, 201-250)(Assam Dragons): a unique sabre-toothed shark mouth on P-40s; flight rudder markings by December 44. Some P-38s during 44. P-51s from late-44. **26th FS** (Yellow; 70-99, 251-300)(China Blitzers): P-40s in China with yellow nose band aft of spinner. P-51 yellow tail stripes added in July 44. **449th FS** (301-350): Activated in the CBI with P-38s in August 43. Attached to 23d FG during 44. Spinners red by 45.

80th FG (X AF)(Burma Banshees): To the CBI with P-40s in May 43. White skull on nose with squadron-color spinners and white tail numbers. P-47s with fuselage numbers, EAC stripes, and squadron-color cowl rings. **88th FS** (10-39). **89th FS** (40-69). **90th FS** (70-99). **459th FS** (100-127, 1-25)(Twin Dragon Squadron): Activated in India with P-38s in September 43. Dragon nacelle/boom markings worn only from early-44 to early-45. Transferred to 33d FG in May 45.

81st FG (XIV AF): Moved from the MTO with P-47s in February 44. The 81st was the one Fourteenth AF group to adopt a version of the EAC stripes on wings, nose, and horizontal tail only; an additional band was added to the fuselage aft of the wing. Aircraft were numbered from 901-1000, and a system of squadron tail bands was adopted. **91st FS**. **92d FS**. **93d FS**: soon moved to India as combat training squadron.

311th FG (X AF, XIV AF): Four A-24/A-36/P-51 squadrons moved to the CBI in August 43 as 311th BG (Dive). Originally carried two-digit tail numbers and squadron-color spinners. In September 43 one squadron was inactivated, with the other three redesignated fighter bomber squadrons; the group became the 311th FBG. All were redesignated fighter units in May 44. Moved to the Fourteenth AF in September 44 carrying squadron tail bands and plane numbers 1001-1100. **385th BS (D)**: disbanded September 43. **528th FS/382d BS (D)**. **529th FS/383d BS (D)** (White). **530th FS/384th BS (D)** (Yellow)(Yellow Scorpions).

476th FG (XIV AF): Activated in China without squadrons or aircraft in May 43; disbanded in July 43.

NIGHT FIGHTERS: Two squadrons of Jet Black P-61s. Evidence of painted cowl gills by mid-45, but color and unit unknown. **426th NFS** (X AF, XIV AF): To the CBI in June 44, to the Fourteenth in November. Returned to the US in November 45. **427th NFS** (X AF, XIV AF): To the CBI in June 44; detached to the Twelfth AF in the MTO in August 44; returned to the CBI in October 44; to Fourteenth AF in August 45.

Pyrotechnics in India on the Fourth of July, 1945 - the 33rd FG expends a little P-38L ammunition by way of celebration. Although the 33rd had left the Fourteenth Air Force the previous September, its aircraft continued to use 800-series identification numbers, such as the "839" on the boom of 44-25749. (USAF)

(Above) Receiving P-51As in late 1943, the 76th FS skewed their shark mouths to fit the new nose contours. Note the radio call number (3608#, with the last digit in shadow) on the aft fuselage; tech orders specified this location if the radio call would not fit the tail. (Ward)

When the 75th FS transitioned to Mustangs in late 1944, the squadron abandoned the shark mouth and adopted black tails with white aircraft numbers between 150 and 199. In mid-1945 the aircraft number was moved to the nose, and the range was changed to 50 through 99. (Bowers)

The 118th TRS brought its Mustangs to the 23rd FG in mid-1944. Most squadron aircraft carried yellow-edged black lightning bolts on their fuselages, with similar markings later added to wing and tail tips. (Muth)

59

A trio of 25th FS P-40Ns display the markings of that squadron's three flights: 220 of B Flight, 239 of C Flight, and 232 of A Flight. (Army)

Shark mouths and yellow tail stripes mark P-51Bs of the 26th FS. Number 264 also carries a flight- or squadron-leader stripe on the rear fuselage. (Army)

Few late-war photos exist of the 16th FS's Mustangs. Aircraft 388 was recorded at Nanning, China, with a dark horizontal tail stripe and dark spinner. (USAF)

(Below) The 80th FG's P-40Ns carried fearsome skull markings. Variations in shape and expression kept any two aircraft from sharing the same design.

The 80th FG commander's P-47, "00," at Myitkyina in 1945. The group insignia is carried beneath the canopy, and the cowl ring is trisected in red, white, and blue. *Miss Nancy Lee* was assigned to the 2nd CCS, 1st CCG. (Army)

(Right) *Miss'-ippi Hone!e!* was a P-38H of the 459th FS, photographed in February 1944. Although later famous as the Twin Dragon Squadron, the 459th wore its famous nacelle markings for only a year. (Army)

(Right) While most modern representations of the 459th FS's nacelle markings show a green head and tongue, with a red mouth, the markings actually applied during World War II used a green head with red lips and tongue, and black mouth. (USAF)

(Below) *HAMMER'S DESTRUCTION CO* was the personal P-38L of 90th FS ace Lt Sam Hammer. Five Japanese flags and simple nickname, with no added unit markings, are a far cry from the flashy schemes of other aces and units. July 1945. (USAF)

Heavy weathering and staining distinguish this 81st FG P-47D. The 81st's variation of Eastern Air Command Stripes was often applied to the horizontal tail also, although the stripes are missing in this instance. (Bowers)

(Left) *BLUE PICKLE* was a P-51D of the 311th FG's 529th FS. The radio call number was repainted on the aft fuselage when yellow and black markings were applied to the vertical tail. The white spinner is in the 529th squadron color. (Bowers)

(Left) Another 311th FG Mustang, *Ginny "B"* was a P-51K of the 530th FS. The squadron color, on the spinner, is unknown. (Bowers)

(Below) A Jet Black 427th NFS P-61A, photographed over Burma in 1945. The radio call number (25628) is in red to lessen contrast. Most P-61s flew without upper turrets in an effort to increase the aircraft's endurance. (USAF)

A 9th BS B-24 over China in January 1945. Each of the 7th BG's squadrons adopted a distinctive checkerboard pattern on the vertical tail. (DMA)

Many B-24s of the 308th BG wore Jet Black under surfaces for night missions. The black and yellow tail markings, adopted in July 1944, identified the 425th BS. (USAF)

BOMBER MARKINGS IN THE CBI

7th BG (X AF): From the SWPA to India in March 42 with two B-17/LB-30 squadrons and two B-25 squadrons. Plane-in-group numbers replaced radio call numbers. The heavy bombers moved to the MTO in mid-42; aircraft which returned wore RAF fin flashes. Conversion to B-24s in late 42. Tail markings applied between October and November 44. **9th BS** (20-39). **11th BS**: B-25s, transferred to 341st BG in September 42. **22nd BS**: B-25s arrived in July 42 and transferred to the 341st BG in September 42. **436th BS** (60-79). **492nd BS** (80-99): Activated in the CBI in October 42. **493rd BS** (40-59): Activated in the CBI in October 42.

12th BG (X AF): B-25s from MTO to India in March 44. Tails marked with two digit numbers. Monster faces painted on many aircraft by November 44. Conversion to A-26s beginning in mid-45. **81st BS** (1-25). **82nd BS** (26-50). **83rd BS** (51-75). **434th BS** (76-99).

308th BG (XIV AF)(The Liberators of China): B-24s to China in early 43, Fourteenth AF tail numbers 451-550. Tail markings beginning in July 44. B-24 shark mouths after November 44. Many Jet Black bellies, some Jet overall. **373rd BS**: Transferred to SWPA (494th BG and 11th BG) from July 45 to January 46. **374th BS**. **375th BS**. **425th BS**.

341st BG (X AF, XIV AF)(Falcon Group, Burma Bridge Busters): Activated India with B-25s in September 42; moved to China in

January 44. Two-digit plane numbers; 400-series numbers in 44. Squadron emblems on most noses. A-26 transition beginning in mid-45. **11th BS** (Jiggs Squadron): From 7th BG in September 42. **22nd BS**: From 7th BG in September 42. **490th BS** (Skull and Wings Squadron): To the CBI in September 42. Some monster-style nose markings. **491st BS** (Ringer Squadron): To CBI in September 42.

402nd BG (XIV AF): Activated in China without squadrons or aircraft in May 43. Disbanded in July 43.

Many 12th BG B-25s and A-26s carried monster faces similar to the one seen on *DOG DAIZE*. The 82nd BS's nose art also tended to include a bulldog derived from the squadron insignia. (Bowers)

Three 341st BG Mitchells on a leaflet dropping mission over China in late-August 1945. The camouflaged B-25J in the foreground carries tail number 443. The uncamouflaged B-25J in the lead has tail number 407 and, on the nose, the emblem of the 11th BS and the nickname *HOOTIN' SHOOTIN' CHARLIE JOHN*. The enigmatic B-25H has tail number 1001! (Army)

TRANSPORT MARKINGS IN THE CBI

64th TCG: As the ARROWHEAD detachment, the **4th, 16th, 17th, 18th, 35th TCS**s were borrowed from the MTO to help relieve Imphal-Kohima between April and June 44. A thin white fuselage band was carried by several of the C-47s.

443rd TCG (X AF): To the CBI in March 44, taking command of four C-47 squadrons already in theater. Two-digit tail numbers in use by November 43. The 27th TCS moved to China in 44; the remaining three squadrons transitioned to C-46s in 45. All moved to China in August 45. **1st TCS** (1-25)(Tiger Fleet): To X AF in February 43. C-46s with white "TIGER FLEET" on fuselage and white cowl flashes. **2nd TCS** (26-50): To X AF February 43. **27th TCS**: To X AF in January 44. Attached to 69th Composite Wing (XIV AF) May 44 to July 45. Two character tail codes (letter "A" and individual aircraft character). **315th TCS** (51-75): To X AF in January 44.

322nd TCS (XIV AF, X AF): Started with one C-47 in April 42 as total transport of the China Air Task Force. Grew to XIV AF Transport Section in March 43, with the famous "Coolie" emblem on C-47 noses. Emblem modified for redesignation as 322nd TCS in September 44 in China; letter "D" and individual aircraft character on tails. Re-equipped with C-46s in 1945, with squadron emblems on tails. Transferred to X AF, August 45-January 46.

1st CCG (X AF): C-47s to India in August 44. Partial re-equipment with C-46s in June 45. Combat Cargo Squadrons renumbered as Troop Carrier Squadrons in September 45. Returned to the US in December 45. **1st CCS/326th TCS** (The Great Snafu Fleet): C-47 and C-46. "The Great Snafu Fleet" painted over C-47 cabin windows. To XIV AF

Four 27th TCS C-47s on a mission over China. When the 27th was attached to the Fourteenth AF in May 1944, its aircraft tails were marked with an "A" and an individual aircraft letter or number. Most C-47 vertical tails were built and painted by subcontractors; the shade variations resulted from different stocks of OD. (USAF)

A 1st TCS C-47A, parked under the hazy skies of China. This aircraft (42-100441) was lost on 13 September 1944. (USAF)

June-December 45. **2nd CCS/327th TCS**: C-47. To XIV AF September-December 45. **3rd CCS/328th TCS**: C-47. White "3" and horseshoe painted on some tails by mid-45. **4th CCS/329th TCS**: C-47 and C-46.

3rd CCG/513th TCG (X AF): Activated in India in June 44 with C-47s. Tails marked with squadron number as Roman numeral and "COM-CAR"; last three digits of serial often highlighted. Transition to C-46s in 1945. Redesignated **513th TCG** in September 45, with squadrons renumbered and redesignated in October 45. Inactivated in China in April 46. **9th CCS/330th TCS**. **10th CCS/331st TCS**. **11th CCS/332nd TCS**. **12th CCS/333rd TCS**: 333rd TCS emblem on C-46 tails.

4th CCG (X AF): To India with C-47s in November 44. C-46 transition in December 44. Inactivated in India in February 46. **13th CCS**. **14th CCS**. **15th CCS** (Smiley's Airlines): "Smiley's Airlines" painted over cabin windows by January 45. **16th CCS**.

ATC MARKINGS IN THE CBI

By March 1942 the Japanese had closed every seaport capable of resupplying the Chinese armies. The Allies planned a tenuous air route to transport materiel from Indian bases through Burma to China, but by May 8th even the Burmese air base at Myitkyina fell to the Japanese. Now transport pilots would be forced to fly from Burma's Assam Valley over the Himalayas to Yunnan Province. By map, it's a reckoning of only 500 miles. But the base at Chabua (near Dinjan) was at ninety feet above sea level, the Chinese terminus at Kunming at about 6,200 feet, and the peaks of the Himalayas in between thrust 10,000 to 18,000 feet high. Pilots named the treacherous obstacle "the HUMP."

Early in 1942 AAF Ferrying Command (AAFFC) was directed to activate one group with three squadrons (75 aircraft) of C-47s or C-53s.

TWENTIETH AIR FORCE TAIL MARKINGS
58th Bomb Wing

40th BG, from Aug 44

25th BS

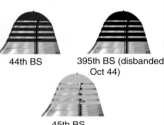

44th BS

395th BS (disbanded Oct 44)

45th BS

40th BG from May 45

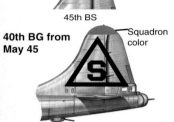

Squadron color

444thBG, from Aug 44

676th BS

678th BS

677th BS

444th BG, from May 45

462d BG, from August 44

768th BS

(Entire Group from October 44.)

769th BS

770th BS

771st BS (disbanded October 44)

462nd BG, from May 45

468th BG, from August 44

792nd BS

793rd BS

794th BS, until Oct 44

795th BS until October 44, 794th BS after October 44

468thBG, from May 45

73rd BW, from Oct 44

497th BG

T 498th BG   V 499th BG   Z 500th BG

73rd BW, from Apr 45

497th BG

T 498th BG   V 499th BG

Z 500th BG

313th BW, from Jan 45

6th BG

X 9th BG   E 504th BG   K 505th BG

313 BW, from Apr 45

6th BG

 9th BG    504th BG

 505th BG

Yellow disc was used by all Groups late in the war

314th BW

19th BG

29th BG

39th BG

330th BG

Yellow letter was used by all Groups late in the war

315th BW

16th BG

331st BG

501st BG

502nd BG

Some blue tail markings late in the War

65

"Luke" was a B-25J converted to a fast transport for the 322nd TCS. The Mitchell has drawn a crowd after landing at Mang-shih (on the Burma road, just over the border in China) in December 1944. (Army)

BACK BREAKER was a C-46 of the 1st TCS - the "TIGER FLEET!" The squadron's white cowl design was not copied by the 443rd TCG's other two squadrons. (McDowell)

(Above) Photographed at Dinjan, India, this is a C-47A of the 10th CCS — carrying "X COM-CAR" in yellow on the tail. Aircraft of the 3rd CCG commonly carried the first section of the radio call in red ("315") with the last three digits in yellow ("794"). (USAF)

Part of the 1st Ferrying Group left for India in April. Operations (under the Tenth Air Force) included transporting fuel for the planned return of Doolittle's Tokyo Raiders, for supplying General Stilwell's retreat through Burma, and for evacuating refugees from China. On 1 December 1942, command of the India-China airlift passed from Tenth Air Force to Air Transport Command (as AAFFC had been redesignated in June). The new command was expected to place a greater emphasis on strategic resupply rather than the Tenth Air Force's stress on combat and combat preparation.

In early 1943 the ATC moved a dozen C-87s to its India-China Division (redesignated India-China Wing in July 44); thirty C-46s also left the US for Karachi in April. The buildup to one of history's most famous (and perilous) airlifts was under way.

In addition to ATC's own units, several Tenth and Fourteenth Air Force groups were placed under India-China Wing control, particularly when the Chinese Army or the Twentieth AF required additional support. During May 44, for example, the 7th BG, 308th BG, 443rd TCG, 3rd and 4th CCGs, and the 2nd and 3rd CCSs were operationally dedicated to increasing the tonnage carried over the Hump. None of these aircraft modified their unit markings as a result of this service, though many carried the camel symbols of "Hump" missions.

Generally, one type of aircraft was assigned to each base under the control of an ATC Army Air Forces Base Unit. Individual aircraft were marked with the last three (or four) of the serial on the nose and enlarged upon the tail, and an ATC decal on the rear fuselage. A system of colored nose flashes may have differentiated units. By early March 1945, one or two initials on the fin designated several bases, and in May or June of 1945 the entire base name, or an abbreviation, was painted on the tail.

(Below) The tail of this 322nd TCS Skytrain carries the AAF's radio call (476458) and the Navy's designation and BuAer number (R4D-6, 50839). (Bowers)

During 1945, the following bases and units came under the control of ATC's India-China Wing:

Barrackpore: 1340th AAFBU with C-54s. Codes: **B'PORE**.
Bhamo: 1358th AAFBU.
Chabua: 1333nd AAFBU with C-46s. Codes: **C, CHAB**, or **CHABUA**
Changan (Hsian): 1354th AAFBU.
Chanyi: 1367th AAFBU with C-46s and C-47s. Codes: **CY CHANYI**.
Chengkung: 1339th AAFBU with C-46s and C-47s.
Dergaon: 1329th AAFBU.
Dinjan: with C-46s. Codes: **DINJAN**
Dum Dum (Calcutta): 1305th AAFBU.
Jiwani: 1306th AAFBU.
Jorhat: 1330th AAFBU with C-87s and C-109s. Codes: **JORHAT**
Karachi: 1306th AAFBU with C-47s. Codes: **K**.
Kunming: 1340th and 1365th AAFBU with C-46s and C-47s.
Kurimitola: 1345th AAFBU with C-54s.
Liuchow: 1363rd AAFBU.
Loping: 1359th AAFBU.
Luliang: 1366th AAFBU with C-46s and C-47s.
Lushien: 1360th AAFBU.
Misamari: 1328th AAFBU with C-46s. Codes: **MISA**
Mohanbari: 1332nd AAFBU with C-46s
Myitkyina: 1348th AAFBU with C-47s.
Shamshernagar: 1345th AAFBU with C-87s and C-109s.
Shanghai: 1369th AAFBU with C-47s. Codes: **SHANGHAI**
Sookerating: 1337th AAFBU with C-46s and C-47s. Codes: **S** or **SOOK**
Tezgaon: 1351st, then 1346th AAFBU, with C-54s. Codes: **TEZGAON**
Tezpur: 1327th AAFBU with C-87s and C-109s.

The **1352nd AAFBU Search and Rescue** at Mohanbari, operated a jungle rescue section. Its L-1s, L-4s, L-5s, C-47s, UC-64s, and B-25s were painted orange-yellow, with black fins and stabilizers and black diagonal underwing stripes.

The **10th Air Jungle Rescue Squadron** at Myitkyina flew similar missions, although its aircraft wore the standard USAAF colors.

The Twentieth AF had three Air Transport Squadrons assigned for its internal transport needs. Two of those squadrons were transferred to ATC: The **2nd ATS** (known as "Sylvester's Circus") flew C-46s, each marked with a large yellow nose flash. The **3rd ATS**, upon moving to ATC, traded its C-46s for C-109s, which it then marked with blue and yellow horizontal nose bands.

A 15th CCS C-46D runs up its engines in Burma in March 1945. The squadron became known as "Smiley's Airlines," an oblique reference to the unit's commanding officer, Major "Smiley" Fields. (USAF)

The airline-style "Assam Air Lines" markings on this ATC C-47A were the trademark of the 1337th AAFBU at Sookerating (note the "S" atop the tail). Other markings were standard for ATC aircraft in the CBI. (USAF)

The 2nd Air Transport Squadron ("Sylvester's Circus") carried large yellow nose flashes on most of its C-46s. This aircraft also has yellow flashes on its engine nacelles. (AFM)

Another Sookerating aircraft, this time an uncamouflaged C-46A. ATC markings practice include repeating the last three or four digits of the radio call number upon the tail and in a small yellow diamond on the nose. (USAF)

FIGHTER MARKINGS

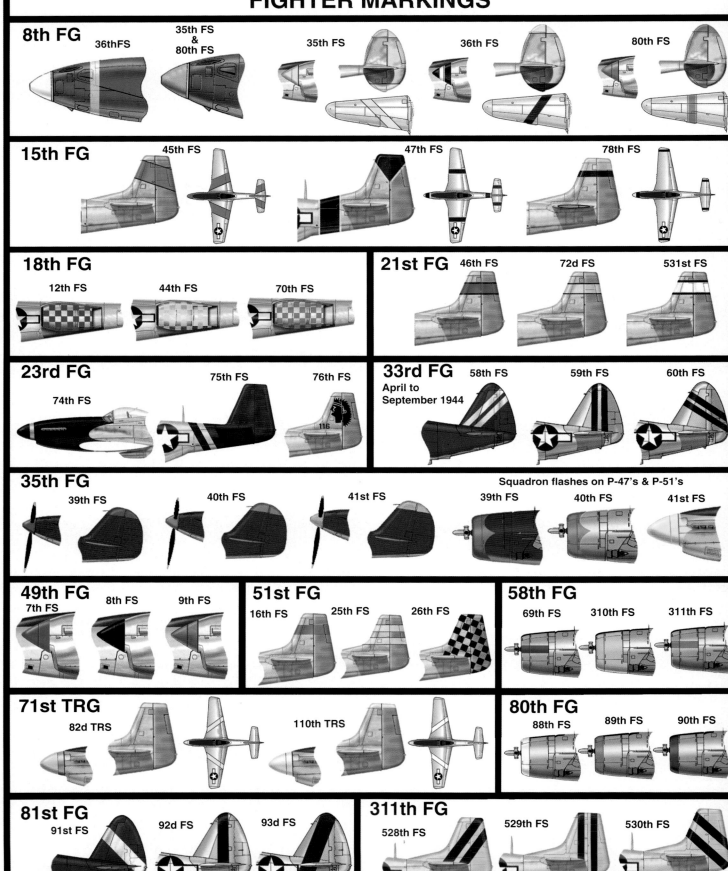

8th FG
- 36thFS
- 35th FS & 80th FS
- 35th FS
- 36th FS
- 80th FS

15th FG
- 45th FS
- 47th FS
- 78th FS

18th FG
- 12th FS
- 44th FS
- 70th FS

21st FG
- 46th FS
- 72d FS
- 531st FS

23rd FG
- 74th FS
- 75th FS
- 76th FS
- 116

33rd FG
April to September 1944
- 58th FS
- 59th FS
- 60th FS

35th FG
- 39th FS
- 40th FS
- 41st FS

Squadron flashes on P-47's & P-51's
- 39th FS
- 40th FS
- 41st FS

49th FG
- 7th FS
- 8th FS
- 9th FS

51st FG
- 16th FS
- 25th FS
- 26th FS

58th FG
- 69th FS
- 310th FS
- 311th FS

71st TRG
- 82d TRS
- 110th TRS

80th FG
- 88th FS
- 89th FS
- 90th FS

81st FG
- 91st FS
- 92d FS
- 93d FS

311th FG
- 528th FS
- 529th FS
- 530th FS

318th FG

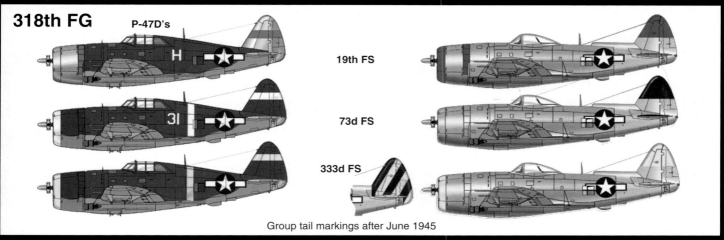

P-47D's

19th FS

73d FS

333d FS

Group tail markings after June 1945

348th FG

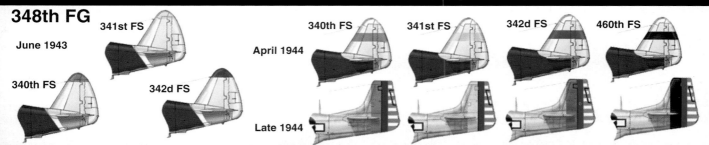

June 1943

341st FS

340th FS

342d FS

April 1944

340th FS   341st FS   342d FS   460th FS

Late 1944

413th FG

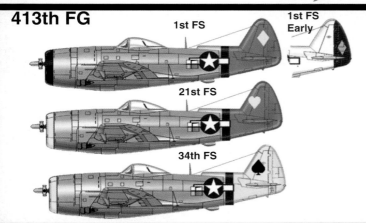

1st FS

1st FS
Early

21st FS

34th FS

414th FG

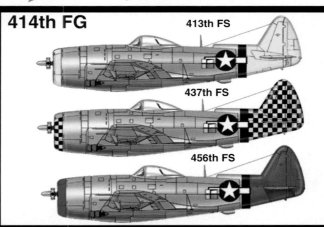

413th FS

437th FS

456th FS

475th FG

431st FS   432d FS   433d FS

507th FG

463d FS   464th FS   465th FS

506th FG

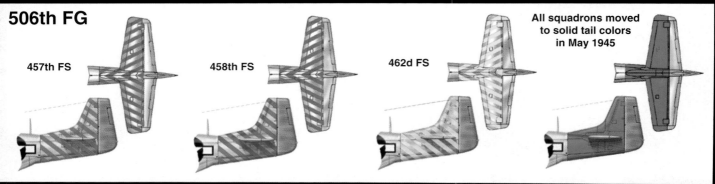

457th FS   458th FS   462d FS

All squadrons moved
to solid tail colors
in May 1945

ATC considered the C-54 its most effective transport; the Skymaster combined four-engine reliability with range, payload, altitude, and speed. This C-54G carries "THE AIR TRANSPORT COMMAND" over the fuselage windows and "ATC" under the left wing. (AFM)

(Left and Below Left) C-109s were B-24s converted into flying gas tankers - a particularly important mission for the resupply of China. Considering the cargo, the crash landing of this 3rd ATS C-109 was relatively uneventful. Number 059 carried numerous personal markings, including 151 camel "Hump mission" symbols. Note also the unpainted prop on engine number 3. (USAF)

(Below) If more than one aircraft carried the same "last three" for its radio call, ATC added an "A" suffix to the tail number. This C-47B was photographed at Shanghai in September 1946. (Bowers)

(Above) *STINKY 2* was an F-5A (42-13301) of B Flight, 9th PRS. Dust and weathering have taken their toll on the Haze Paint camouflage scheme. The radio call number has not been applied to the tail, although the last three digits are in black on the nose. (USAF)

RECONNAISSANCE MARKINGS IN THE CBI

8th PRG (X AF): To India in March 44 using F-5s, F-6s, F-7s, and P-40s. Became the 8th RG in June 45. Returned to the US in November 45. **9th PRS**: Moved haze painted F-4s and F-5s to the CBI in March 42; flight-color spinners and last two or three of the radio call repeated on the nose or nacelle. One B-25 assigned to each flight. Assigned to 8th PRG in April 44. Large individual aircraft letter painted on the tail by mid-44; smaller twin tail letters and three thin boom bands worn by late 44. **20th TRS**: To the CBI in January 44 with unmarked P-40s and B-25s and (in 1945) F-6s. Transferred to 8th PRG April 44. **24th CMS**: Synthetic-Haze-painted F-7s to the CBI in January 44. Emblem on tail. **40th PRS**: To CBI with uncamouflaged F-5Es in July 44. Field-applied Synthetic Haze paint, late 44.

11th PG: Assigned to the Second AF in the USA. F-7 detachments from the 1st PRS and 3rd PRS mapped sections of the CBI in 43 and 44. Markings are unknown.

21st PRS (XIV AF)(China Falcons): F-4s and F-5s moved to the CBI in June 43. Plane numbers 550-599 painted on the boom radiators. Fronts of spinners and nacelles painted yellow by 45. Some F-6s in 45.

35th PRS (X AF, XIV AF): F-5s to the CBI in May 44. Emblem on most noses; XIV AF tail numbers 800-850.

(Below) *Miss Virginia E* was an F-5B (42-67375) also with B Flight of the 9th PRS. The camouflage here is Synthetic Haze Paint, with the leading edges of the outboard wing panels in unpainted aluminum (repainting was frequently ignored after leading edge fuel tanks were installed). Again, there is no radio call number on the tail, although the last three digits are on the nose in yellow. (USAF)

(Below) Taxiing at Pandaveswar, India, in early 1943, much of this 9th PRS F-4 has been weathered down to the black undercoat. (Bowers)

(Above) Another 9th PRS Lightning, this time an uncamouflaged F-5E. Although not visible in this view, the radio call (tail) number exhibited a common Lockheed application error: the fiscal year (43) was ignored, and only the last five digits (28600) were displayed. The 9th painted a small black "KK" above the radio call as an individual aircraft marking. Note that the anti-glare panels are dull dark green, and the gear struts and gear door inside surfaces are Neutral Gray. (USAF)

BOMBER MARKINGS

3rd BG
8th BS
13th BS
89th BS
90th BS

312th BG
386th BS
387th BS
388th BS
389th BS

417th BG
672nd BS
673rd BS
674th BS
675th BS

5th BG
Oct 44

Band May be in Squadron color

23rd BS
31st BS
72nd BS
394th BS

7th BG
9th BS
436th BS
493rd BS

2nd PCS

20th CMS

11th BG
26th BS
42nd BS
98th BS
431st BS

22nd BG
2nd BS
19th BS
33rd BS
408th BS

30th BG
27th BS
38thBS
392nd BS
819th BS

43rd BG
63rd BS
64th BS
65th BS
403rd BS

868th BS

90th BG
319th BS
320th BS
321st BS
400th BS

72

307th BG
Group HQ
370th BS
371st BS
372nd BS
424th BS

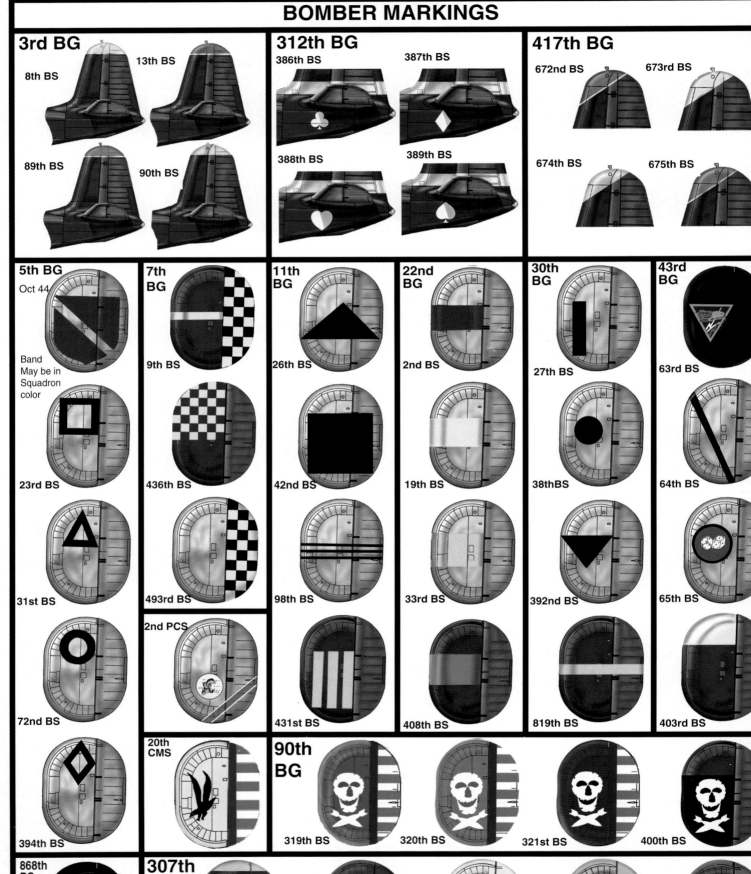

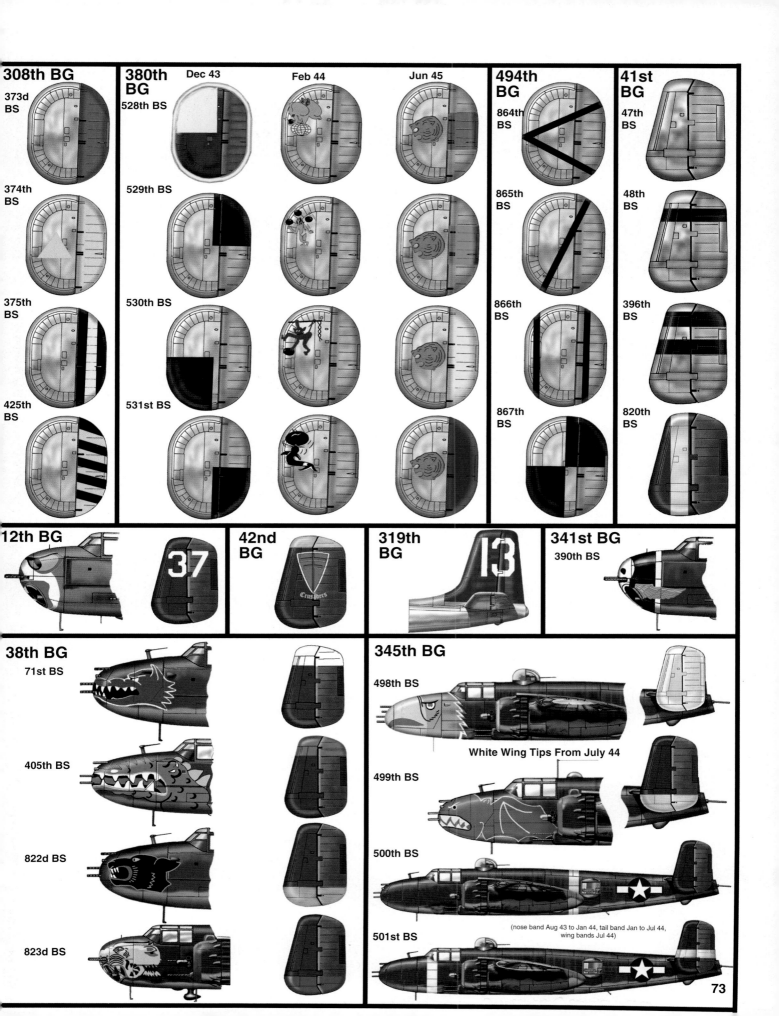

308th BG

373d BS

374th BS

375th BS

425th BS

380th BG

528th BS
Dec 43

529th BS

530th BS

531st BS

Feb 44

Jun 45

494th BG

864th BS

865th BS

866th BS

867th BS

41st BG

47th BS

48th BS

396th BS

820th BS

12th BG

37

42nd BG

Crusaders

319th BG

13

341st BG

390th BS

38th BG

71st BS

405th BS

822d BS

823d BS

345th BG

498th BS

White Wing Tips From July 44

499th BS

500th BS

501st BS

(nose band Aug 43 to Jan 44, tail band Jan to Jul 44, wing bands Jul 44)

AIR COMMANDO MARKINGS IN THE CBI

1st ACG (X AF): The Air Commandos moved to India as **Project 9** in November 43, becoming the **5318th Provisional Unit** in December 43, and the **1st ACG** in March 44. Originally aircraft were organized in sections: Bomber Section with B-25s; Fighter Section with P-51As; Light Plane Section with L-1s, L-5s, and R-4s; Transport Section with C-47s; Glider Section with CG-4s and TG-5s; and Light Cargo Section with UC-64s. P-51s, B-25s, and C-47s were marked with five white diagonal fuselage stripes. Additionally, C-47 tails displayed a black "?" on a white disc. The group left combat in May 44, dropped the bomber section, replaced the P-51s with P-47s, and, in September 44, reorganized with squadrons. Fuselage stripes, which had fallen out of use during the reorganization, reappeared by February 45, including a smaller representation on the fin strakes of gliders and liaison planes. Fighter squadrons trained in Merlin-engined P-51s from May to October 45. **5th FS (Commando)**, **6th FS (C)**, **164th LS (C)**, **165th LS (C)**, **166th LS (C)**, **319th TCS (C)**.

2nd ACG (X AF): Moved to India from September to November 44. Responding to the 1st ACG's "?" marking, the 2d punctuated its tails with a "!" marking. Fighters and liaison aircraft also marked fuselages and wings with black EAC bands and lightning bolts. **1st FS (C)**: P-51s. **2nd FS (C)**: P-51s. **127th LS (C)**: C-64s, L-1s, L-4s, and L-5s. Transferred to XIII AF on Okinawa in September 45;

The first YR-4B (42-107237) was one of several R-4 helicopters assigned to the 1st ACG for combat trials. Camouflage was OD and Neutral Gray, with no unit markings applied. A shark mouthed L-5 (42-98418) sits to the right. (USAF)

The Flying Abortion was an aptly named 1st ACG P-47D; it was cobbled up from several other aircraft, including an 81st FG aft fuselage and a camouflaged left wing. The aircraft was photographed in Shanghai in December 1945. (Bowers)

to VII AF October to November 45. **155th LS (C)**: C-64s, L-4s, and L-5s. Transferred to V AF on Okinawa in September 45. **156th LS (C)**: C-64, L-4s, and L-5s. Transferred to V AF on Okinawa in September 45. **317th TCS (C)**: C-47s and CG-4As. Transitioned to C-46s in 1946.

(Above) Wrecked on landing, this B-25G carries the white fuselage stripes of the 5318th Provisional Unit, bomber section. The Mitchells remained with the 1st ACG for only two months after that unit activated in March 1944. (USAF)

Maintenance under spartan conditions; P-47Ds of the 5th FS are repaired in March 1945. EAC stripes mark wings and tails, without covering elevators or rudders. Individual aircraft numbers were painted under the cockpits. (AFM)

(Right) The 1st ACG's 319th TCS included several C-45s for light cargo duty. Five blue fuselage stripes were the only unit markings. (Bowers)

(Right) While the 1st ACG limited use of its "?" tail marking to C-47s, the 2nd ACG painted its "!" tail markings on most group aircraft. This Northwestern-built CG-4A was photographed enroute to Burma in February 1945. (USAF)

Three 2nd AGC C-47As move supplies into Rangoon on 1 May 1945. The 2nd's exclamation point was a sly imitation of the question mark carried by 1st ACG C-47s. (USAF)

Billy's Filly, **P-38L of Lt William Fowkes,**
12th FS, 18th FG, Zamboanga, Philippines.

Billy's Filly

SEARCH AND RESCUE

59 91
315 991

Chardie

1352d AAFBU Search
and Rescue

ChardiE, **C-47A, 1352d AAFBU Search and Rescue,**
Mohanbari, Assam, 1945

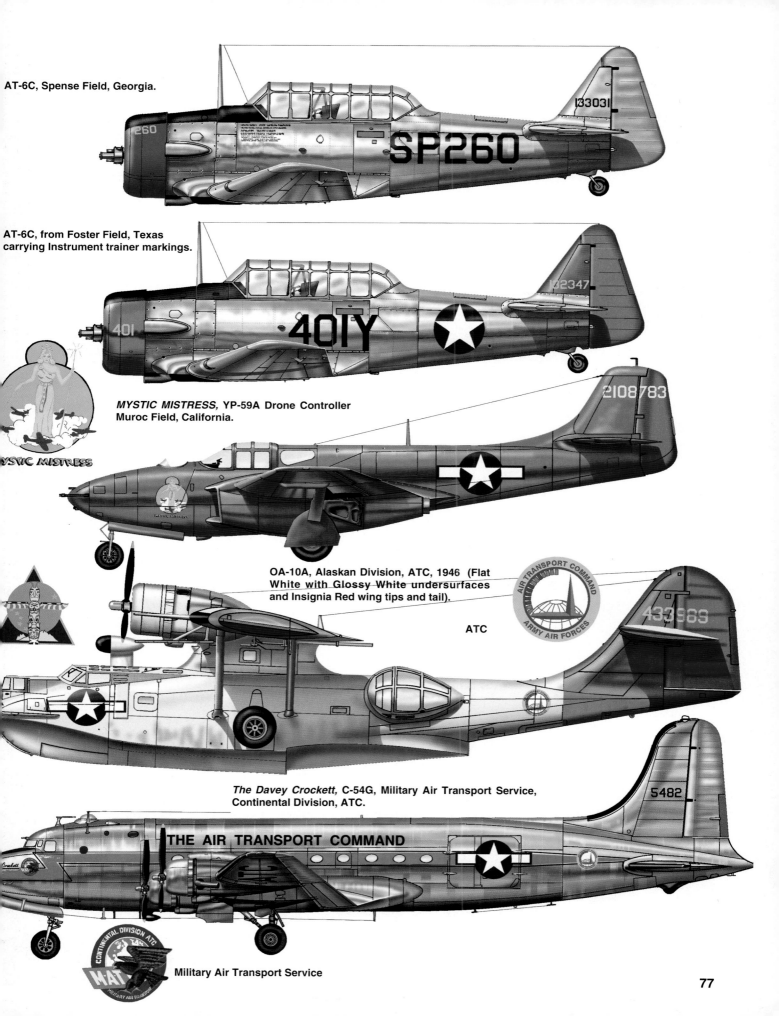

AT-6C, Spense Field, Georgia.

133031

SP260

AT-6C, from Foster Field, Texas carrying Instrument trainer markings.

132347

4OIY

MYSTIC MISTRESS, YP-59A Drone Controller Muroc Field, California.

2108783

MYSTIC MISTRESS

OA-10A, Alaskan Division, ATC, 1946 (Flat White with Glossy White undersurfaces and Insignia Red wing tips and tail).

ATC

AIR TRANSPORT COMMAND
ARMY AIR FORCES

433989

The Davey Crockett, C-54G, Military Air Transport Service, Continental Division, ATC.

5482

THE AIR TRANSPORT COMMAND

CONTINENTAL DIVISION ATC
MATS
MILITARY AIR TRANSPORT

Military Air Transport Service

77

(Above) A 2nd ACG P-51D in India, February 1945. Along with the exclamation mark, the group markings include black lightning bolts on the fuselage and wings. (Bowers)

(Above Left and Left) *Little Indian* was one of the few operational Mustangs to carry Bazooka tubes. By mid-1945, enlarged aircraft numbers have replaced the exclamation point and EAC band on the vertical tail. Note the small ace of diamonds marking on the nose. (Bowers)

(Below) 2nd ACG L-5s, including this mud-splattered L-5B (44-17065), carried black markings similar to the fighters. The bolts on the wings are a close match, while the fuselage band descends rather than rises. Liuchow, July 1945. (USAF)

MISCELLANEOUS UNIT MARKINGS IN THE CBI

1st LG (Prov) (X AF): This provisional unit formed in August 44 to control the X AF's two liaison squadrons; a third squadron was added in November 44. Aircraft carried white plane-in-group tail numbers. The group was never formally activated, disbanding in April 45. **5th LS** (1-25): To the CBI with L-1s, L-4s, and L-5s in March 44. To X AF in August 44. **71st LS** (26-50): To the CBI with UC-64s, L-1s, L-4s, and L-5s in July 43. To XIV AF in July 45. **115th LS** (51-75): To the CBI in October 44 with L-1s, L-4s, and L-5s. To the XIV AF in July 45.

Chinese-American Composite Wing (XIV AF): The CACW was formed as part of the Chinese Air Force in October 1943. Crews could be Chinese or American; for operations the CACW reported to the XIV AF's 68th Composite Wing. Aircraft usually carried US insignia and were numbered in sequence with other XIV AF units. The three provisional CACW groups were

1st BG (M)(P) (Gambay Group). **1st BS (M)(P), 2nd BS (M)(P), 3rd BS (M)(P), 4th BS (M)(P).**

3rd FG (P). 7th FS (P), 8th FS (P), 28th FS (P), 32nd FS (P).

5th FG (P). 17th FS (P), 26th FS (P), 27th FS (P), 29th FS (P).

This converted B-17 was assigned to General Frank Hackett of the Bengal Air Depot. The BAD insignia (colors unknown) on the nose comprises a Bengal Tiger and air depot spearhead upon a disc. Note the red, white, and blue prop tips and, on the right rear fuselage, the modified hatch/step. (USAF)

(Above) The 803rd Air Evacuation Squadron repainted this C-47A as *"AMBULANCE PLANE No 1"* in December 1943. The liberal application of white squares and red crosses was unique for a CBI Skytrain. The radio call tail number was "232836," with the last three digits repeated above in larger characters. (USAF)

(Above) The Tenth Air Force used several OA-10 Catalinas for clandestine operations. *Smokey,* carrying an ASV antenna and under wing tanks, wears a camouflage scheme of unknown origin. Palal, India, March 1945. (USAF)

Flagship of the Skull & Wings served with the HQ Squadron of the 341st BG. Barely visible on the aft fuselage are the four yellow and three black stripes applied to dozens of bombers at Karachi. The purpose of this marking remains unclear. (USAF)

Buzz Boy IV, P-51D of flight leader, Capt William G. Burlingame, 41st FS, 35th FG, Johnson AB, Japan, 1947.

78
474233

BUZZ BOY IV

41st FS

431st FS

Palpitatin Pal, P-51D, 431st FS, 475th FG, Tachikawa, Japan, 1947.

129
472655

PALPITATIN PAL

Rhapsody In Rivets

Rhapsody In Rivets, P-80A of Group CO Col Bruce K. Holloway, 412th FG, 1946 transcontinental flight.

18
16
6
485069

PN-069

Cosmic Ray Research
ARMY AIR FORCES
BARTOL RESEARCH FOUNDATION
NATIONAL GEOGRAPHIC SOCIETY

"OLE MISS" VI

"OLE MISS" VI, B-29, AAF All Weather Flying Center, August, 1946.

521793

Cosmic Ray Research
ARMY AIR FORCES
BARTOL RESEARCH FOUNDATION
NATIONAL GEOGRAPHIC SOCIETY

port side

Starboard side

58" WING
5 9

58" WING

Dave's Dream, Silverplate Project B-29, 509th Bomb Group, Kwajalein. (On 1 July 1946 *Dave's Dream* dropped the first atomic bomb of Operation Crossroads over Bikini Lagoon).

509th BG, 58th Wing

58th Wing

B
354
7354

A 115th LS L-5 over Burma in December 1944. The only unit marking is the white plane-in-group number "55" on the tail. (USAF via Eich)

(Above) CACW group commanders Col T. Alan Bennett and Major C. H. Yaun pose with Major W. L. Turner. The P-40s in the background carry Chinese national insignia and Fourteenth Air Force aircraft numbers. (USAF)

(Below) A 2nd BS (P), 1st BG (P), B-25H over Neisiang on 2 April 1945. The aircraft carries US national insignia and, on the nose, the Fourteenth Air Force number "609." (USAF)

Aviation historian/photographer Peter Bowers recorded this Droop Snoot P-38J at Calcutta in April 1945. His notes describe the camouflage as OD with sky blue undersides. The radio call number, in black, was 2104154. (Bowers)

(Above Left and Left) This P-38L Droop Snoot, was the personal aircraft of General Stratemeyer, commander of the AAF in India-Burma. The General's three-star placard can just be seen inside the clear nose. (Bowers)

(Below) The Army Airways Communications Service converted this C-46 into the "Loran School of the Air" to help instruct navigators in the use of the Loran radio navigation system. (USAF)

B-29s Against Japan

XX Bomber Command was activated in the US in November 1943 to train B-29 crews for the long-range strategic bombing of Japan. Early in 1944 HQ XX BC and the 58th BW moved to India to prepare staging bases in the CBI. But when the Twentieth Air Force was activated on 4 April, its headquarters remained in Washington: commanded by AAF Chief "Hap" Arnold, XX AF was expected to remain free of CBI politics. Attacks on the Japanese home isles began in June.

Following XX Bomber Command's move to India, XXI BC was activated in March 1944 to continue the training of B-29 crews and units. By October, the first XXI BC B-29s were moving to the Marianas Islands, followed by HQ XXI BC in December, and the four CBI groups in April 1945. HQ XXI Bomber Command was terminated on 16 July 1945 and redesignated HQ Twentieth Air Force. By August, twenty-one groups in five bomb wings were delivering explosives, incendiaries, and two nuclear devices to Japan.

At the end of the European War the Eighth AF began relocating to Okinawa without personnel, equipment, or combat units. B-29s and crews of the Eighth's 316th BW would arrive before the war's end, but would see no combat.

Although the majority of B-29s were delivered without camouflage, the early airframes were OD and Neutral Gray. With stainless steel an innovation on B-29s, Materiel Command worried that standard paints and primers (designed for aluminum skins) would not adhere properly. Tests proved special primers unnecessary, and about fifty camouflaged B-29s were accepted. The initial 58th BW CBI compliment included about two dozen camouflaged B-29s. Before leaving the US, most aircraft received new aluminum-doped rudders; the only CBI Superfortress to retain an OD rudder was YB-29 41-36963, used by the 462nd BG as a fuel transport.

On 12 November 1943, the B-29 (and the P-38) became the USAAF's first aircraft ordered in natural metal. Unpainted B-29s did not carry nose or nacelle antiglare panels, though many 73rd BW Superforts wore a black antiglare ring around the dorsal sighting blister. Jet Black under surfaces were later applied in the Marianas to many Superforts assigned night missions. In June 1945 the Marietta factory began painting Jet Black under surfaces on its B-29Bs, but none of the factory paint jobs arrived in the Pacific by VJ-Day.

Soon after arriving in the Marianas, the first two XXI BC wings adopted geometric tail markings with group designator letters.

Target: Yawata. China-based B-29s of the 40th BG prepare for the first mission against Japan, 15 June 1944. Aircraft were identified solely by radio call numbers until group markings were developed in August. (USAF)

The 73rd BW carried a small hollow square with the group letter above and two-digit aircraft numbers below. 313 BW arrived and used a small triangle instead of a square. The 314th BW, which moved to Guam between December 1944 and February 1945, may have briefly introduced similar markings, using a small circle.

On 13 April 1945, XXI BC published a listing of enlarged tail markings for improved recognition. The groups of the 58th BW, now arriving from the CBI, were included in the new system. Squadrons would now paint individual aircraft numbers on the aft fuselage, and command planes would carry a short black bar on the tail over the aft ventral gun turret. The 13 April order may have been preceded by another directive, since documents and photos establish that several units were applying the new markings before 3 April.

Twentieth Air Force fighters (the 15th, 21st, 414th and 506th FGs) are covered in the Pacific Basin chapter starting on page 24. Groups are listed below in wing order, and tail markings are reproduced on page 65.

58th BW

In the CBI the 58th BW was amalgamated into XX BC in mid-July 1944, and formally deactivated in mid-September. Groups began applying unit markings of their own designs in August 1944. Each four-squadron group reorganized with three squadrons in October. The 58th was reactivated in February 1945, taking all four groups to West Field, Tinian, during April. Tail markings changed to a large 58th BW triangle enclosing a group letter, although some vestiges of the CBI markings were still evident in June 45. (Note the unusual ranges of aircraft numbers.)

40th BG: Squadron-color tail tips and stripes with individual aircraft letters in the CBI. Tail tip colors retained in Marianas. Group *Kagu Tsuchi* nose emblem by July 45. **25th BS** (1-12, 40, 43), **44th BS** (14-26, 42, 44), **45th BS** (27-38, 41), **395th BS** (Black): inactivated in October 44.

444th BG: CBI tail marking of small diamond with plane number. Lead B-29 markings of a small black disc on the tail. Squadron-color fuselage band added October 44, with lead ships carrying diagonal stripes in the bands. Fuselage bands were retained in the Marianas, with engine access panels in same colors. (Mid-45 squadron number ranges listed.) **676th BS** (Green, 10-24), **677th BS** (Red, 50-64), **678th BS** (Yellow, 30-44), **679th BS**: disbanded in October 44.

462nd BG (The Hellbirds): Individual tail letters and squadron

Another 40th BG Superfortress, this time over Rangoon in November 1944. The tail tip and four horizontal stripes are yellow, the squadron color of the 45th BS. The aircraft is nicknamed *Eddie Allen* in memory the Boeing flight test engineer killed in the XB-29. (USAF)

A 462nd BG B-29 rests on its nose in India following an electrical malfunction in January 1945. The large "2" on the fin designates the 462nd BS, as does the yellow rudder (though the group had begun painting all rudders red in October 1944). The large "N" was the individual aircraft letter. (USAF)

(Below) In the CBI, 444th BG markings used a simple aircraft number inside a black diamond; early squadron number ranges are unclear. From October 1944, a squadron-colored band encircled the waist aft of the wing. (USAF)

OD-camouflaged B-29 were a rarity in the CBI; 42-6241 was one of about two dozen. Stripped of its turrets, this aircraft hauled gas over the Hump with the 40th BG in mid-1944. Note the aluminum-doped rudder, a replacement fitted to most B-29s in the US. (USAF)

colored rudders in CBI. Group red rudder (carried through V-J Day) and squadron ID number (1, 2, or 3) on the fin after September 44. "Hellbirds" nose emblem added in the Marianas. **768th BS** (#1, 2-16), **769th BS** (#2, 20-33), **770th BS** (#3, 40-53), **771st BS**: Disbanded in October 44.

468th BG (Billy Mitchell Group): Two diagonal squadron-colored rudder bands carried in the CBI. Squadron-colored star painted on both sides of noses in October 44; comet tails added to the stars later in the month. Group emblem placed on tail in January 45, moved to the nose in April 45. Squadron-color tail tips on Saipan. **792nd BS** (1-16), **793rd BS** (21-35), **794th BS** (41-54), **795th BS**: disbanded in October of 1944.

73rd BW

Moved to Isley Field, Saipan, between August and October 44. In May 45, personal nose art was ordered removed and replaced with a black and yellow spear and globe, with approved nicknames painted in the spear's shaft.

497th BG: **869th BS** (1-20), **870th BS** (21-40), **871st BS** (41-60).
498th BG: **873rd BS** (1-20), **874th BS** (21-40), **875th BS** (41-60).
499th BG: **877th BS** (1-20), **878th BS** (21-40), **879th BS** (41-60).
500th BG: **881st BS** (1-20), **882nd BS** (21-40), **883rd BS** (41-60).

313th BW

Moved to North Field, Tinian, in December 1944. Three of the wing's lead B-29s briefly carried a solid black disc on the tail in April 1945. Group-color cowl access panels were carried from February 1945; group-color tail tips from May 1945. Lead B-29s wore black/yellow/black fuselage bands.

6th BG: The group's pirate emblem replaced individual nose art after May 1945. **24th BS** (1-20), **39th BS** (21-40) **40th BS** (41-60).

9th BG: Group insignia added to the right side of the nose by July 1945. **1st BS** (1-20), **5th BS** (21-40), **99th BS** (41-60).

504th BG: Late-war use of group nose emblem with yellow banner. **398th BS** (1-20), **421st BS** (21-40), **680th BS** (41-60).

505th BG: Squadron emblems with green and white banners reported

as late-war nose markings. **482nd BS** (1-20), **483rd BS** (21-40), **484th BS** (41-60).

509th Composite Group: The unit that dropped the atomic bombs commanded a single bomb squadron. **393rd BS** (71 to 95): A plain black arrowhead (no circle) was assigned as the group tail marking before arrival on Tinian in May 1945; instead, the arrowhead within the 73rd BW's ring was briefly carried. Group B-29s were soon camouflaged with the tail markings of other units; after VJ-Day the arrowhead in circle returned. **320th TCS** (Green Hornet Airlines): C-54s with squadron emblem and green bird wing on nose.

314th BW

Moved to North Field, Guam, beginning in December 1944. There is some evidence of small circle tail markings similar to other early XXI BC symbols. By April 1945 markings were revised to a solid black square with group letter. (Group letters were often painted yellow to cover other markings.) The 314th globe and banner emblem was added to the right side of noses beginning May 1945. Aircraft number and group letter were repeated on cowls.

19th BG: By March 45, a small group letter "A" was applied to many tails. Postwar unit markings included the group emblem on the left nose and the last four of serial in large characters on the tail. **28th BS** (1-20), **30th BS** (21-40), **93rd BS** (41-60).

29th BG: **6th BS** (1-20), **43rd BS** (21-40), **52nd BS** (41-60).

39th BG: **60th BS** (1-20), **61st BS** (21-40), **62nd BS** (41-60).

330th BG: **457th BS** (1-20), **458th BS** (21-40), **459th BS** (41-60).

315th BW

To Northwest Field, Guam, in April/May 1945. Some group tail markings apparently were filled in with medium blue. Many aircraft wore jet black undersides.

16th BG: **15th BS** (1-20), **16th BS** (21-40), **17th BS** (41-60).

331st BG: **355th BS** (1-20), **356th BS** (21-40), **357th BS** (41-60).

501st BG: **21st BS** (1-20), **41st BS** (21-40), **485th BS** (41-60).

502nd BG: **402nd BS** (1-20), **411th BS** (21-40), **430th BS** (41-60).

316th BW

The Eighth AF's 333rd and 346th BGs arrived on Okinawa between July and August 1945. Their B-29s returned to Tinian on 12 August

Two diagonal squadron-colored rudder bands marked B-29s of the 468th BG. *Bengal Lancer* has the blue starred comet and bands of the 793rd BS, the comet tail is painted in orange and yellow tiger stripes. December 1944. (USAF)

(Above) When the 58th BW relocated to Tinian in April 1945, tail markings were changed to a group letter in a black triangle. *Journey for Margaret* carried the "N" of the 444th BG, with the nose insignia and an aircraft call number (29) from the 678th BS. The squadron's yellow/black fuselage band is repeated on the outboard engine cowls. Iwo Jima, July/August 1945. (D. T. Britt)

Coral Queen under repair on Saipan. Tail markings comprise a small square (representing the 73rd BW), a letter "A" (designating the 497th BG), and an individual aircraft number "8" (for the 869th BS, which was assigned the range 1 to 20). (USAF)

Another 73rd BW Superfortress shares the wing's hollow square tail marking, with the "T" of the 498th BG. After adding the unit markings to the fin, the group repainted the last four digits of the serial number on the rudder. Work progresses on the nose art; the aircraft was eventually nicknamed *Fay*. (USAF)

From April 1945 the 73rd BW tails carried black group letters standing almost twelve feet high. At the same time, all XX AF B-29s added a forty-two-inch-high aircraft number to the aft fuselage; the 73rd repeated the number on the nose in two-foot-high characters. (USAF).

The 6th BG's *Flak Alley Sally* force-landed on Iwo Jima following a March 1945 mission to Kobe. The 313th BW triangle marking was worn over the radio call number, with the group letter above it. Red cowl panels were a further marking of the 6th BG. (USMC)

1945; on the 14th 32 B-29s readied for a strike on Fumaya, but combat operations were suspended the same day. The 2 September show of force over the Tokyo surrender ceremonies included 24 316th B-29s. While plans for wartime markings remain a mystery, the VIII AF insignia was painted on tails early in 1946.

Transports

The 1st, 2nd, and 3rd Air Transport Squadrons (Mobile) were assigned to XX BC in China in July 1944, and a provisional C-109 unit was formed in August. The need for dedicated strategic transport was countered by the difficulties of operating the units, so all C-109s and two of the air transport squadrons were turned over to the India-China Division of ATC in October 1944. The **1st Air Transport Squadron (Mobile)** was retained, following the B-29s to the Marianas. 1st ATS C-46s wore a skull and crossed bones nose motif with a horizontal white tail band. Additionally, the 509th CG included the C-54s of the **320th TCS.**

Reconnaissance

1st PRS: One F-13 detachment moved to the CBI in 1944. No unit markings known.

3rd PRS: F-13s to the Pacific in November 1944; B-24s added later. Initial markings of a small "F" at the tail top. In common with all squadrons assigned directly to HQ XX AF, tail tips were painted black in April 1945.

41st PRS: F-5Gs with black tail tips on to Guam in June 1945. Plane numbers from 1 to 25 on boom radiators. Spinner fronts in flight colors.

55th RS (Long Range, Weather): Weather recon B-24s moved to the Western Pacific in January 1945 as the 655th BS. The unit was redesignated 55th RS in June. While the squadron emblem was carried on some tails, there is no evidence the unit used black tail tips.

(Left) Pre-April 1945 markings for the 314th BW remain unconfirmed. However, shortly after arriving on Guam, most 19th BG B-29s received a small "A" at fin top. The small circle marking seen on several 29th BG aircraft may have been intended as a 314th BW marking. (USAF)

(Below) After April 1945 the 313th BW marked its tails with an eleven-foot-diameter circle. Black group letters were painted inside the circle, and group colors painted on tail tips and cowl panels. *Look Homeward Angel* carries the "pirate" nose markings common to 6th BG B-29s after June. 11 August 1945. (USAF)

(Above) In April 1945 the 314th BW adopted larger tail markings with an unpainted group letter inside a solid square. The 314th would later repaint the group letter in yellow, increasing visibility and covering vestiges of the radio call number. Guam, 14 April 1945. (USAF)

A B-29 of an unidentified unit prepares for a mission in June 1945. The aircraft honors the 3rd Marine Division by carrying that unit's insignia on its nose. (USMC)

The same aircraft was photographed while in storage at Pyote Field, Texas after the war. Under surfaces had been repainted with Jet Black for low-level night missions. (Cavanagh)

(Below) The 315th BW was the last Twentieth Air Force wing to enter combat. Equipped with B-29Bs, the 315th was assigned the diamond tail markings, with group letters ("B" designating the 16th BG). The 315th appears to have begun painting blue in the interior of its tail markings by war's end. (USAF)

Junior was an F-5B of the 28th PRS; The black tail included a white diamond with the individual aircraft letter "J." The squadron insignia is painted on the nacelle. (USAF)

(Left) This C-46A was assigned to the Guam Air Depot, a Marianas support facility. The small arrowhead over the radio call is yellow with a blue border and blue "GAD" in the center. (USMC)

(Left) Lockheed F-5Gs of the 41st PRS carried their aircraft number on the boom radiators and flight colors on the spinner fronts. Fin tops were black, reflecting assignment to Headquarters XX AF. (Lloyd)

The only Twentieth Air Force air transport squadron to move from the CBI to the Marianas was the 1st ATS (Mobile). Squadron markings included a white skull and crossed bones at the nose and a black-bordered white band on the tail. (D.T. Britt)

(Above and Above Right) Another support organization, the 655th Bomb Squadron, operated B-24Ls such as *Weather Witch* (44-49506), seen here in May 1945. The 655th was redesignated the 55th Recon Squadron (Long Range, Weather) in June; the photo to the left is a later view of the tail, with squadron insignia added. Although assigned to Headquarters XX AF, 55th aircraft apparently never carried black tail tips. (USAF/Osbourne)

(Right) The 3rd PRS flew F-13s and a few F-7s and radar mapping B-24s (a radome has been installed aft and right of the bomb bay. The HQ XX AF black tail top is applied to outer surfaces only. (D.T. Britt)

(Right) The AAF's 230 OA-10As Catalinas were built by Canadian Vickers, and most were accepted with the RCAF scheme of flat white upper surfaces and sides with gloss white under surfaces; the anti-glare panel was RAF Slate Gray. While most aircraft were later repainted, this 4th ERS Catalina remains all white. Unit markings were not carried by the 4th. (D.T. Britt)

(Below) March 1944 saw the formation of HQ AAF Pacific Ocean Areas (AAFPOA), a logistical support organization for VII AF and XXI BC reporting directly to the Commander in Chief, Pacific Ocean Areas (CINCPOA). Photographed on Saipan in June 1944, this LB-30 was used by the Deputy Commander of XX AF and the Navy's Commander Forward Area. The nose emblem was likely that of AAFPOA. (USAF)

POSTWAR USAAF TO USAF

The end of World War II brought a rapid reduction in the Army Air Forces' capabilities. By July 1946 only 52 groups were listed as active, and only two of those were considered combat ready! The AAF also began to redesign its chain of command. The wartime combat organizational hierarchy ran from the numbered *air force* through functional *command*, *division* (in larger air forces), *wing*, *group*, and *squadron*. From March 1946 major commands would become the first level of authority below HQ USAAF; commands which were previously subordinate to numbered air forces were eliminated. That March saw three new commands: Air Defense Command (ADC), which was responsible for defense of the US; Strategic Air Command (SAC), which was responsible for strategic bombing missions; and Tactical Air Command (TAC) which was responsible for domestic tactical aircraft, including tactical transports, at a time when most domestic units were reserve organizations. Air Transport Command remained intact, responsible for strategic airlift. Training Command became Air Training Command on 1 July 1946. The Air National Guard, a reserve organization with operational units assigned to state governments, came into being in September 1947. Overseas, Far East Air Forces (FEAF) remained in control of units in the Philippines and Occupied Japan; the US Strategic Air Forces in Europe had become US Air Forces in Europe in August 1945; the Eleventh Air Force had become Alaskan Air Command in December 1945; Sixth Air Force became Caribbean Air Command in July 1946; and Seventh Air Force became Pacific Air Command in December 1947.

The National Security Act of 1947 created the Department of the Air Force (to be headed by a Secretary of the Air Force) on 26 July 1947. Directly under the Department of the Air Force, the United States Air Force (headed by the Chief of Staff, USAF) was created. The first Secretary of the Air Force was installed on 18 September 1947 (the date considered the USAF's birthday), and the first Chief of Staff on 26 September. The USAF was now separate from the Army, with an equal voice at the cabinet level. The Cold War was coming, and that voice would be have to be heard through many challenges...

In November 1945 the AAF ordered the application of a new system of identification markings to all fixed-wing aircraft (not helicopters or lighter-than-air aircraft) operating solely in the Continental USA. Known only as identification markings in technical orders, the markings

This aircraft, the second XP-84 (45-59476), set a US speed record of 611 mph on 8 September 1946. The puttied and sanded skins of many early jets were painted overall Aircraft Gray The large black Buzz Numbers guaranteed easy identification. (USAF)

quickly became known popularly as "Buzz Numbers." While photo versions of most aircraft (such as the F-10 photo version of the B-25) received Buzz Numbers, reconnaissance aircraft such as the F-11, F-12, and F-14, which were not expected to remain in the US, were exempted from the regulations.

Buzz numbers were to be placed below the left wing, in characters the same height as the national insignia. The fuselage star returned to its proper place on all fuselage sides (including on Training Command aircraft); the codes were to be carried in the largest remaining practical space, with characters between 32"x48" and 8"x12". Technical orders called for yellow characters on dark aircraft, black letters on light aircraft, and red letters on black-camouflaged aircraft. Buzz Numbers were based on the aircraft type and serial. Two letters, the first for designation and the second a model equivalent, preceded the last three digits of the serial number. For example, AT-6 serial 42-43850 would carry Buzz Number TA-850 (**T** for trainer, **A** from a chart as the model equivalent of the AT-6, and the last three digits of the serial). When aircraft with the same identification numbers were assigned to a base, suffix letters could be added for clarity. If AT-6s serialled 42-43850, 42-85850, and 44-80850 had shared a home station, they would have been marked TA-850, TA-850A, and TA-850B. Buzz Numbers continued to be used in service until the early 1960s.

In January 1947 the national insignia was changed by the addition of a red bar. The change itself is often associated with the creation of the USAF, but it was actually a joint Army/Navy revision. The thickness of the red bar would frequently be misinterpreted during application, a mistake that continues to be made fifty years later. By design the white bar was to be split into three equal parts, one red and two white, each one-sixth the radius of the star itself. The common and continuing error has resulted in the red bar being added in the same thickness as the blue border surrounding the insignia - *one-eighth* of the radius of the star. The thinner red bar left thicker white bars above and below.

The three months after formation of the USAF saw the release of at least one major revision to markings technical orders. No copy of that TO has surfaced in recent years, so the effect of the revisions cannot be known; photos from the last three months of 1947, however, do not show any noticeable changes.

The 412th FG, the AAF's original P-80 group, was redesignated 1st FG in July 1946. These 412th aircraft are overall Aircraft Gray, with tails and nose caps in unidentified squadron colors. The application of Buzz Numbers had not yet been standardized. (USAF)

IDENTIFICATION MARKINGS (BUZZ NUMBERS)

AA-XXX - A-24	BL-XXX - B-44	CP-XXX - C-78	LC-XXX - L-4	GG-XXX - CG-15 **	PQ-XXX - P-82
AB-XXX - A-25	BM-XXX - B-36*	CQ-XXX - C-82	LD-XXX - L-5	PA-XXX - P-38	PR-XXX - P-83
AC-XXX - A-26	CA-XXX - CQ-3	CR-XXX - C-87	LE-XXX - L-6	PB-XXX - P-39	PS-XXX - P-84
AD-XXX - A-31	CB-XXX - C-43	CS-XXX - C-97	LF-XXX - L-14	PC-XXX - P-40	TA-XXX - AT-6
AE-XXX - A-41	CC-XXX - C-45	CT-XXX - C-99	OA-XXX - OA-9	PD-XXX - P-42	TB-XXX - AT-7
BA-XXX - B-17	CD-XXX - C-46	CU-XXX - C-117	OB-XXX - OA-10	PE-XXX - P-47	TC-XXX - AT-11
BB-XXX - B-19	CE-XXX - C-47	FA-XXX - F-2	OC-XXX - O-47	PF-XXX - P-51	TD-XXX - AT-21
BC-XXX - B-24	CF-XXX - C-48	FB-XXX - F-5	OD-XXX - O-60	PG-XXX - P-55	TE-XXX - BT-13
BD-XXX - B-25	CG-XXX - C-49	FC-XXX - F-6	OE-XXX - PB-2B	PH-XXX - P-58	TF-XXX - PT-13
BE-XXX - B-26	CH-XXX - C-53	FD-XXX - F-7	GA-XXX - PG-2	PJ-XXX - P-59	TG-XXX - PT-17
BF-XXX - B-29	CJ-XXX - C-54	FE-XXX - F-9	GB-XXX - PG-3	PK-XXX - P-61	TH-XXX - PT-19
BG-XXX - B-32	CK-XXX - C-60	FF-XXX - F-10	GC-XXX - CG-4A **	PL-XXX - P-63	TJ-XXX - PQ-8
BH-XXX - B-37	CL-XXX - C-64	FG-XXX - F-13	GD-XXX - CG-10A **	PM-XXX - P-75	TK-XXX - PQ-14
BJ-XXX - B-39	CM-XXX - C-69	LA-XXX - L-2	GE-XXX - CG-13 **	PN-XXX - P-80	
BK-XXX - B-42	CN-XXX - C-74	LB-XXX - L-3	GF-XXX - CG-14 **	PP-XXX - P-81	

Sources: TO 07-1-1B, 6 November 1945 and (**) TO 07-1-1, 7 June 1946

* The B-36 assumed this buzz range out of sequence in the summer of 1947, rather than force the repainting of numbers on other aircraft still in inventory.

Under ATC, the Air Rescue Service painted its domestic rescue helicopters Orange Yellow overall. This R-5D was photographed in April 1947. (Larkins)

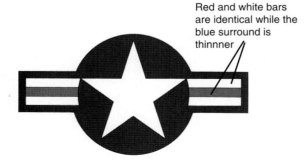

Red and white bars are identical while the blue surround is thinnner

January 1947

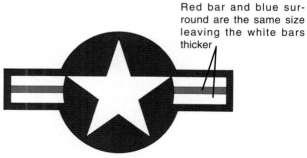

Red bar and blue surround are the same size leaving the white bars thicker

**Common Application
Error For Red Bar**

The 43rd BG was reactivated under the Strategic Air Command in October 1946. SAC tail markings evolved from the Twentieth Air Force's wartime markings. This B-29A was photographed in May 1947. (Larkins)

International Orange was the high-visibility color favored for many test aircraft, including the XS-1 (X-1). Carried aloft by a modified B-29, the XS-1 was the first aircraft to exceed the speed of sound. (USAF)

The All Weather Flying Center developed equipment and techniques to improve flight safety during hazardous weather. AWFC aircraft, such as the XB-19A, carried yellow-bordered nose and wing tips, yellow cowls and spinners, and red tails with yellow chevrons. (Bowers)

The Landing Aids Experiment Station developed and evaluated instrument landing systems. This C-47D carries the station's International Orange flash from nose to tail. While the Buzz Number is not black, the actual color is unknown. (Larkins)

ATC's Pacific Division adopted these blue and gold airline-style markings after the war. "ATC" is painted below the left wing in black; Fairfield, the California home base, is painted below the radio call number. Few ATC aircraft carried Buzz Numbers, since most were expected to leave the US to perform their missions. (Larkins)

Standard Air Rescue Service markings included a yellow fuselage band, yellow wing tips, and yellow upper mid-wing sections. On low- and mid-winged rescue aircraft (such as the C-47 and the B-17) the yellow center section connected over the top of the fuselage. Black bands bordered the yellow areas. (Bowers)

Remotely controlled B-17s wore this scheme for the Crossroads nuclear tests in 1946. Wing tips, tails, and fuselage bands were yellow with black fuselage and tail stripes. The number of stripes was coded to each aircraft's radio control frequency. (USAF)

This AT-6F has enough markings variations to satisfy any enthusiast! The red bar of the national insignia is thinner than specified, and the small Buzz Number lacks a hyphen. The recruiting advertisement was one of several common messages in the post-war AAF. (Larkins)

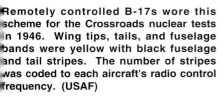

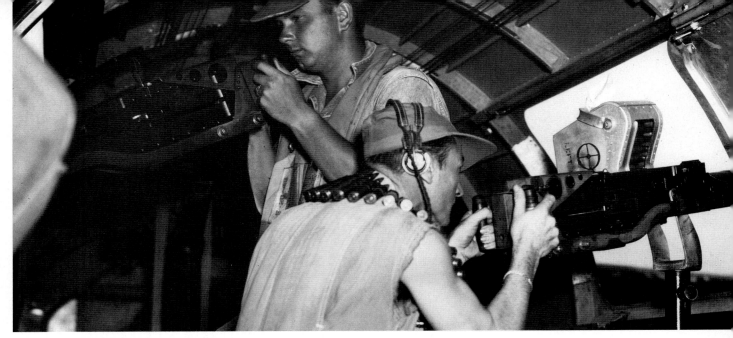

INTERIOR COLORS

The AAF treated its aircraft interiors to protect surfaces and to reduce glare. The simplest coating was a thin translucent film of zinc chromate ($ZnCrO_4$) primer; zinc chromate would protect metal surfaces without adding a major weight penalty, but its cool yellow hue was unsuitable whenever visibility or reflections were an issue. Untinted zinc chromate (or "yellow zinc chromate") was useful for protecting metal when color was unimportant. It was used for radio compartments, gun bays, engine fittings and panels, and (on aircraft such as the P-47) wheel wells.

In 1937 the Air Corps had evaluated a tinted primer for interiors. A formula of one gallon of zinc chromate primer, one-tenth gallon of black enamel, and four ounces of aluminum paste resulted in a dirty yellow green (which, without the aluminum paste, was named "Interior Green" in 1943). Interior Green would originally be specified only for open cockpits, cockpits with sliding covers, and passenger compartments on transports. (It was also used as a second primer coat, since the green could easily be distinguished from the initial yellow coat.) For antiglare purposes, including exterior antiglare panels, closed cockpits and seats, the Air Corps continued to rely on Quartermaster color 9, flat Bronze Green. Ceilings and sides above windows were expected to be left in untreated aluminum.

In late March 1940 the Naval Aircraft Factory began work on an Army-Navy camouflage standard for a dull Dark Green. Working with Monsanto, they produced an enamel chip based on a lacquer chip of Dark Green 30. No joint camouflage standard resulted, but superior low reflectance properties commended Dull Dark Green for use in cockpits

The interior of this B-24 nose turret is Flat Black; however Dull Dark Green was far more common prior to 1945. (USAF)

The waist gun position on a B-17E. Interior skin, ribs, and stringers are zinc chromate (yellow). The interior of the sliding hatch is unpainted. (Color identifications for these photos come from wartime Kodachromes.) (USAF)

and anti-glare panels. Although Dull Dark Green soon began replacing Bronze Green (appearing in some revised specs in late 1940), both colors remained in use for several years.

The use of Dull Dark Green and Bronze Green meant that most cockpits were not painted Interior Green. Aircrew, scanning the skies for friends and foe, could not afford to have cockpit reflections obstructing the view. Specifications changed again in November 1943 with the requirement that interior surfaces visible to crew members and subject to the direct sunlight should be painted Medium Green; surfaces not directly visible, but still casting reflections in cockpit glass (for example, the decking behind P-51D pilot seats) would be painted Flat Black. Flat Black was also standard for instrument panels, radios, and most switch boxes. By 1944 Dark Olive Drab and Flat Black were also being used for anti-glare panels and some cockpits..

Although not listed as an interior color in general specs, Neutral Gray often appears in the specs for certain aircraft. The paint was applied in the wheel wells and bomb bays and on the gear struts of aircraft such as the B-29 and the P-38.

With so many interior colors in use, there are no solid rules for how the interior of any single aircraft was painted. Records and color photos can indicate probable colors, but standards often conflicted, and color photos reveal widespread inconsistencies, even on aircraft of the same type.

The aft interior of this late B-24 is unpainted aluminum. Yellow paint, not zinc chromate primer, was used as a color-code for the oxygen bottles. (USAF)

APPENDIX:
THE COLORS

Color matches for Army 3-1 colors appeared in the first volume of Air Force Colors, while ANA (Army-Navy Aircraft) camouflage colors were explained in the second volume. In Volume III we present the ANA gloss colors. Again we compared the chips to Federal Standard 595 (this time FS 595b) to locate the closest current approximate equivalent. For many reasons, exact equivalents are not always possible - FS 595 is only a collection of Federally approved colors (not a true color system) and many World War II colors were not included.

The arrival of new color standards did not signal the end of old standards. Existing paint stocks would usually be depleted first; occasionally the new standards would be ignored. In Volume II we noted the problem of the Corps of Engineers standard for Olive Drab replacing the AAF standard for Dark Olive Drab in ANA color chips. The Air Force felt that Olive Drab was too light for their purposes, but the move to uncamouflaged aircraft negated their argument. Recently discovered correspondence shows that as late as November 1945 the AAF was advising some paint manufacturers to disregard the ANA standards and produce Olive Drab paint to match their Dark Olive Drab 41 chips.

Over the decades since World War II, many veterans have forgotten the markings painted on the tails of their aircraft. Markings on the nose, however, are usually easier to recall . (USAF)

ANA Color	FS 595 match	Notes
Light Blue No. 501	15102	Good match, 501 was the source for the FS color
Insignia Blue No. 502	15044	Good match, 502 was the source for the FS color
Light Green No. 503	14187	Good match, 503 was the source for the FS color
Olive Drab No. 504	14064	This is only the best equivalent of 504, which is yellower than 14064
Light Yellow No. 505	13591	Good match
Orange Yellow No. 506	13538	Good match
Aircraft Cream No. 507	13523	507 is slightly redder than 13523
International Orange No. 508	12197	Good match, 508 was the source for the FS color
Insignia Red No. 509	11136	Good match, 509 was the source for the FS color
Maroon No. 510	10075	510 is slightly redder than 10075
Insignia White No. 511	17875	Good match. 17875 appears whiter that 511
Aircraft Gray No. 512	16473	Good match, 512 was the source for the FS color
Engine Gray No. 513	16081	Good match, 513 was the source for the FS color
Instrument Black No. 514	27038	Good match
Gloss Black No. 515	17038	Good match, but 515 is not as glossy as 17038

Air Force Colors

Volume One

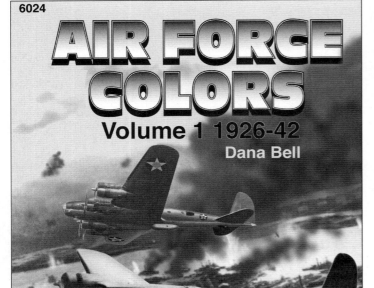

Volume Two

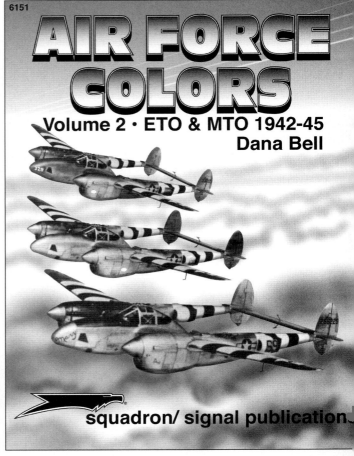

Along with Volume 3, Dana Bell's meticulously researched trilogy presents a library of material that brings into focus the colors and markings used by the Army Air Forces during WW2. What is addressed only in fragments by previous works, this virtual encyclopedia provides a plethora of previously unknown information. Containing 96 pages with over 250 photos and 16 pages of color art work in each volume, Air Force Colors is a must on the book shelves of any enthusiast of the U.S. Army Air Forces during World War II. The artwork is done by the noted aviation and military artist Don Greer.

To receive our latest catalog send $1.00 for postage and handling to:

squadron/signal publications, inc.
1115 Crowley
Carrollton, TX
USA 75011-5010